Power Maths

Year 5 Textb

Series Editor: Tony Staneff

Astrid

Astrid is brave and confident.

She is not afraid to make mistakes.

curious

Ash

flexible

Flo

determined

Dexter

helpful

Sparks

Pearson

Contents

Your teacher will tell you which page you need.

Let's get started!

How to use this book

These pages make sure we're ready for the unit ahead. Find out what we'll be learning and brush up on your skills!

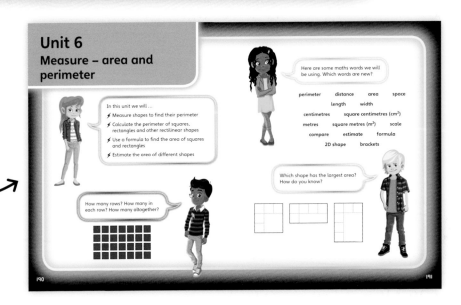

Discover

Lessons start with **Discover**.

Here, we explore new maths problems.

Can you work out how to find the answer?

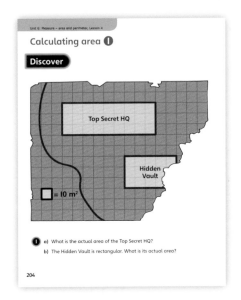

Don't be afraid to make mistakes. Learn from them and try again!

Share

Next, we share our ideas with the class.

Did we all solve the problems the same way? What ideas can you try?

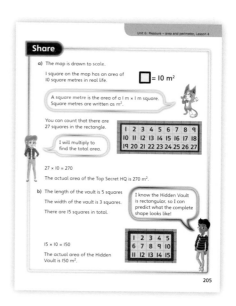

Think together

Then we have a go at some more problems together. Use what you have just learnt to help you.

We'll try a challenge too!

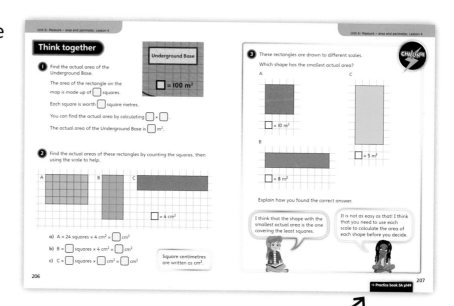

This tells you which page to go to in your **Practice Book**.

At the end of each unit there's an **End of unit check**. This is our chance to show how much we have learnt.

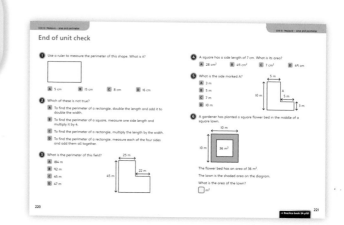

Unit 1
Place value within 100,000

In this unit we will …

⚡ Find the value of each digit in numbers to 100,000

⚡ Partition numbers in different ways

⚡ Round numbers

⚡ Compare and order numbers up to 100,000

⚡ Represent numbers in different ways, including with Roman numerals

In Year 4, we used a place value grid and counters to represent numbers. What number does this show?

Th	H	T	O
1,000 1,000	100 100 100	10 10 10 10	1

We will need some maths words. Which of these have you met before?

ones (Is) tens (I0s) hundreds (I00s)

thousands (I,000s) ten thousands (I0,000s)

place value partition estimate

round compare order equivalent

greater than (>) less than (<) convert

We will also use part-whole models and number lines. What number do these both represent?

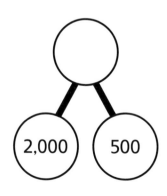

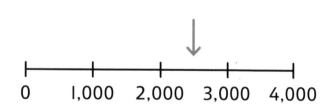

Numbers to 10,000

Discover

1 **a)** Lee hooks eight ducks in total. The last duck he hooks has the value 100.

What is Lee's total score?

b) Olivia also hooks eight ducks.

Her total score is 3,122.

What are the missing scores on the two ducks?

8

Share

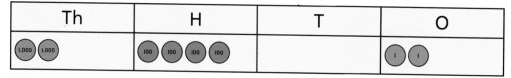

I will use a place value grid. There are no 10s, so I will use 0 as a place holder in the 10s position.

a) Lee hooks eight ducks. Each duck has a value of 1,000, 100 or 1.

Th	H	T	O
1,000 1,000	100 100 100 100		1 1

There are 2 thousands, 4 hundreds and 2 ones.

2,000 + 400 + 2 = 2,402

Lee's total score is 2,402.

b) Olivia's total score is 3,122.

This is made up of 3 thousands, 1 hundred, 2 tens and 2 ones.

Th	H	T	O
1,000 1,000 1,000	100	10 10	1 1

2,000 + 100 + 10 + 2 = 2,112

Th	H	T	O
1,000 1,000	100	10	1 1

The place value counters show there are only 2 thousands, 1 hundred, 1 ten and 2 ones.

Count on another 1,000 to 3,112 and another 10 to 3,122.

You need 1 more thousand and 1 more ten so the missing scores on the two ducks are 1,000 and 10.

Think together

1 **a)** Bella uses place value counters to represent her score for eleven ducks.

Th	H	T	O
1,000 1,000 1,000 1,000		10 10 10 10	1 1 1

What is Bella's score?

There are ☐ thousands, ☐ tens and ☐ ones.

☐ + ☐ + ☐ = ☐

Bella's score is ☐.

b) Bella hooks another two ducks with 1,000 on each.

What is her score now?

Bella's new score is ☐.

2 Zac hooks ten ducks.

His total score is 5,212.

What are the missing scores on the three ducks?

Th	H	T	O

The missing scores are ☐, ☐ and ☐.

3 Aki hooks ten ducks to make a 4-digit number.

a) Which of the following numbers could he have made?

7,210   2,351   8,000   4,222   5,302

b) What other different total scores could he get?

c) What is the highest possible score?

d) What is the lowest possible score?

I will start with scores with only 1 thousand.

I wonder if using a place value grid will help to organise my thinking.

Th	H	T	O

11

Rounding to the nearest 10, 100 and 1,000

Discover

	Bella the Brave	Mo the Magnificent
Game 1	3,425	2,895
Game 2	5,144	5,831
Game 3	7,205	Still to play

1 **a)** Round Bella's score in Game 1 to the nearest 10 and to the nearest 100.

b) Mo's score for Game 3 rounds to 7,000 when rounded to the nearest 1,000.

What could he have scored?

Share

a) Bella scores 3,425 in Game I.

I will find the multiples of 10 that the number lies between when I round to the nearest 10.

I will find the multiples of 100 when I round to the nearest 100.

3,425 is half-way between 3,420 and 3,430.

Bella's score of 3,425 rounds up to 3,430 to the nearest 10.

Look at the Is digit to round to the nearest 10.

A number with 5 or more Is rounds **up**.

Look at the 10s digit to round to the nearest 100.

A number with 0, 1, 2, 3 or 4 tens rounds **down** because it is closer to the previous 100.

3,425 is closer to 3,400 than to 3,500.

Bella's score of 3,425 rounds down to 3,400 to the nearest 100.

b) Mo's score for Game 3 rounds to 7,000 to the nearest 1,000.

The number could be more or less than 7,000.

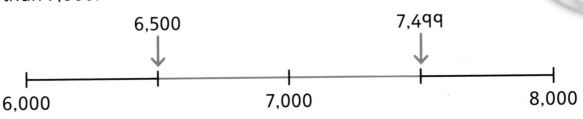

I will try thinking about the largest and smallest numbers that round to 7,000.

The smallest possible number is 6,500 because 5 hundreds rounds up to the next 1,000.

The largest possible number is 7,499 because 4 hundreds round down to the previous 1,000.

Mo's score could be any number from 6,500 to 7,499.

Think together

Bella the Brave

Game 2 5,144

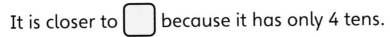

1 **a)** Round Bella's score to the nearest 100.

5,144 is between the numbers 5,☐00 and 5,200.

It is closer to ☐ because it has only 4 tens.

5,144 rounds to ☐ to the nearest 100.

b) Round Bella's score to the nearest 1,000.

5,144 is between ☐,000 and ☐,000.

It is closer to ☐ because it has 1 in the 100s position.

5,144 rounds to ☐ to the nearest 1,000.

2 The base 10 equipment represents one of the children's scores in **Discover**.

a) Whose score is represented?

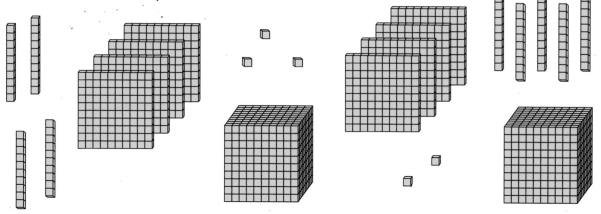

The base 10 equipment represents _____'s score of ☐.

b) Round the score to the nearest 10.

The score is closer to ☐.

☐ rounds to ☐ to the nearest 10.

---

3 Here is Bella's score in Game 4, but two of the digits are missing.

Bella says, 'My score rounds to 5,000 to the nearest 1,000.'

Mo says, 'The last three digits of Bella's score rounded to the nearest 100 are 380.'

What is Bella's score?

Score __,3_5

I will work out one digit at a time. I will start by working out the 1,000s digit.

15

10,000s, 1,000s, 100s, 10s, and 1s

Discover

1 **a)** What does the digit 7 represent each time in the number that shows how many passengers flew with the airline?

b) Show the number of bags on a part-whole model.

Now write the number of bags in words.

Share

a) 72,378 passengers flew with the airline.

The digit 7 appears in two positions in the number 72,3**7**8.

> I will start by representing the number on a place value grid. Then I can see which columns the 7 is in.

TTh	Th	H	T	O
10,000 10,000 10,000 10,000 10,000 10,000 10,000	1,000 1,000	100 100 100	10 10 10 10 10 10 10	1 1 1 1 1 1 1 1

The digit 7 is in the 10,000s position and in the 10s position.

The digit 7 represents 70,000 and 70.

> TTh stands for ten thousands

b) The airline carried 50,624 bags.

The part-whole model for 50,624 is

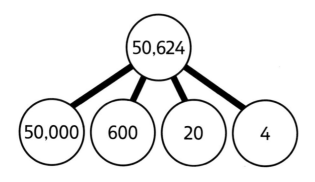

> I will read the number out loud to check.

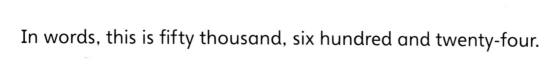

In words, this is fifty thousand, six hundred and twenty-four.

Think together

1   a) The number of bicycles is represented
        on the part-whole model.

        What are the missing numbers?

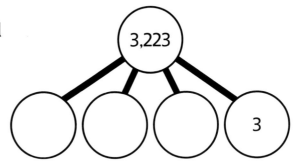

b) Represent the number of skis on a place value grid.

TTh	Th	H	T	O

Say the number and write it in words.

What is the value of the digit 3?

The value of the digit 3 is ⬚.

2   This place value grid represents a number.

TTh	Th	H	T	O
10,000 10,000 10,000 10,000	1,000 1,000 1,000 1,000 1,000 100 100			1 1 1 1 1 1

a) What is the number?

    Say, write and represent the number in as many ways as possible.

b) How many more than 45,000 is the number?

    The number is ⬚ more than 45,000.

3 Max is making some numbers on a place value grid.

TTh	Th	H	T	O
10,000 10,000 10,000 10,000 10,000 10,000 10,000	1,000 1,000	100 100 100	10 10 10 10 10 10 10	1 1 1 1 1 1 1 1 1

a) Which two multiples of 10,000 does the number lie between?

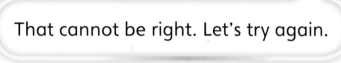

I know it lies between 60,000 and 80,000 because I say 60,000, 70,000, 80,000 when I count in steps of 10,000.

That cannot be right. Let's try again.

b) What other numbers could Max make between 70,000 and 80,000? What is the same? What is different about the numbers?

Explain how you know.

→ Practice book 5A p12

10,000s, 1,000s, 100s, 10s, and 1s ②

Discover

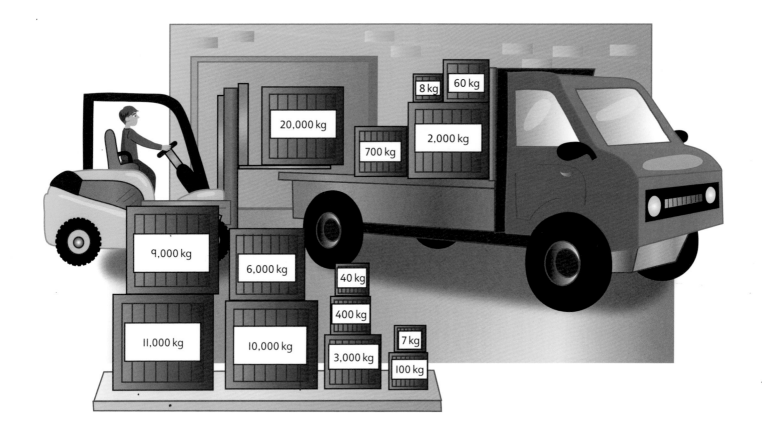

1 **a)** What is the total mass of the five crates on the lorry?

b) Another lorry is loaded with some of the other crates in the picture.

The total mass is 19,140 kg.

Which crates are on this lorry?

Share

a) The five crates on the lorry have the masses 2,000 kg, 60 kg, 8 kg, 700 kg and 20,000 kg.

> I will put the values for the crates into a place value grid.

TTh	Th	H	T	O
10,000 10,000	1,000 1,000	100 100 100 100 100 100 100	10 10 10 10 10 10	1 1 1 1 1 1 1 1

There are 2 ten thousands, 2 thousands, 7 hundreds, 6 tens and 8 ones.

20,000 + 2,000 + 700 + 60 + 8 = 22,768

The total mass of the five crates on the lorry is 22,768 kg.

b) 19,140 kg has 1 ten thousand, 9 thousands, 1 hundred and 4 tens. There are no ones.

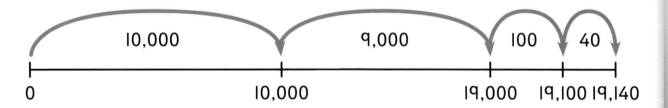

The number line shows how 19,140 is partitioned.

The crates on the lorry could be 10,000 kg, 9,000 kg, 100 kg and 40 kg.

There could also be five crates: 10,000 kg, 6,000 kg, 3,000 kg, 100 kg and 40 kg. The total mass is **equivalent**, but looks a little different.

> I think there is another way! I know 6,000 kg and 3,000 kg also total 9,000 kg.

Think together

1 The number 43,245 is represented on this place value chart.

TTh	Th	H	T	O
10,000 10,000 10,000 10,000	1,000 1,000 1,000	100 100	10 10 10 10	1 1 1 1 1

Partition the number in different ways.

$43,245 = \boxed{} + 3,000 + \boxed{} + \boxed{} + 5$

$43,245 = \boxed{} + 10,000 + \boxed{} + \boxed{} + 40 + \boxed{}$

$43,245 = \boxed{} + 13,000 + \boxed{} + \boxed{}$

$43,245 = 43,000 + 200 + \boxed{}$

2 This number line shows how 23,407 is partitioned.

Write the matching addition sentence.

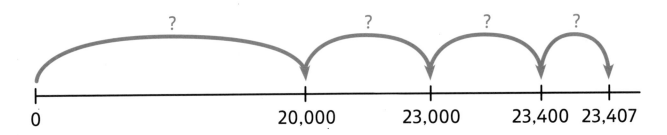

$23,407 = \boxed{} + \boxed{} + \boxed{} + \boxed{}$

3 A lorry is loaded with 26,030 kg.

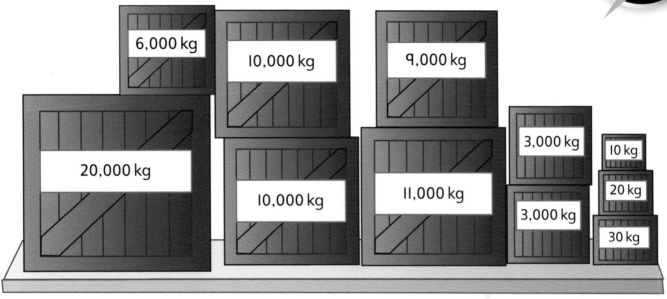

Which of the different crates in the picture could be on the lorry?

Try to find at least **four** different solutions.

I am going to try different combinations of crates to find those that total 26,030 kg.

I wonder if there is a better way. Maybe I could start by partitioning 26,030.

23

The number line to 100,000

Discover

Where does the number 55,000 appear on the number line?

1. **a)** Describe the position of 55,000 on the number line.

   b) Now think about the numbers 53,000 and 56,200.

   Which two multiples of 10,000 are they between?

   Estimate their positions.

24

Share

a) There are lots of ways to describe where 55,000 is on the number line:

> 55,000 is more than half-way along the number line.

> 55,000 lies between two multiples of 10,000.

> 55,000 is 5,000 more than 50,000.

> 55,000 is half-way between 50,000 and 60,000.

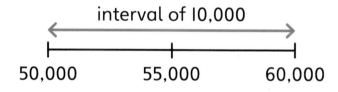

interval of 10,000

50,000   55,000   60,000

> The number line is marked in intervals of 10,000. I will think about how far 5,000 is along the interval of 10,000.

b) 53,000 is between 50,000 and 60,000 because it is 3,000 more than 50,000.

56,200 is also between 50,000 and 60,000. It is 6,200 more than 50,000.

55,000 is half-way between these multiples of 10,000, so 53,000 is less than half-way and 56,200 is more than half-way.

Their positions on a number line are approximately as shown below.

> I divided the gap of 10,000 into 10 equal parts of 1,000 to help me to position the numbers.

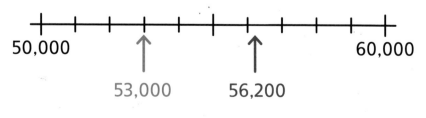

50,000   60,000

53,000   56,200

Think together

1

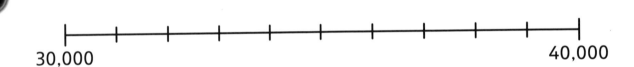

Which numbers do points A, B and C represent?

Point A is about ☐ because it is half-way between ☐ and ☐.

Point B is about ☐ because it is half-way between ☐ and ☐.

Point C is about ☐ because it is half-way between ☐ and 85,000.

2

30,000 ├──┼──┼──┼──┼──┼──┼──┼──┼──┤ 40,000

a) What is the value of each of the small marks on the line?

The numbers are ☐ , ☐ , ☐ , ☐ , ☐ , ☐ , ☐ , ☐ and ☐.

b) Explain where to position the number 37,500.

It should be half-way between ☐ and ☐.

c) Estimate where to position the numbers 30,500 and 34,500 on the number line.

3 Is point A, B, C or D the best estimate for 14,432 on this number line?

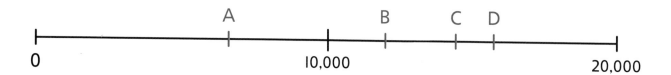

The best estimate for 14,432 is ☐ .

Explain your thinking to your partner.

4

- I am thinking of a 5-digit number between 60,000 and 70,000.
- My number is more than half-way between 60,000 and 70,000.
- It is closer to 70,000 than to 65,000.
- The 1,000s digit is even.

Alex

a) Write down at least three numbers that Alex can be thinking about.

b) Write down a number more than half-way between 60,000 and 70,000 that Alex cannot be thinking about.

I know that 60,500 is half-way between 60,000 and 70,000. I will look for numbers that are larger than 60,500.

I do not think that is right. 60,500 is half-way between 60,000 and 61,000. I will think again.

27

→ Practice book 5A p18

Comparing and ordering numbers to 100,000

Discover

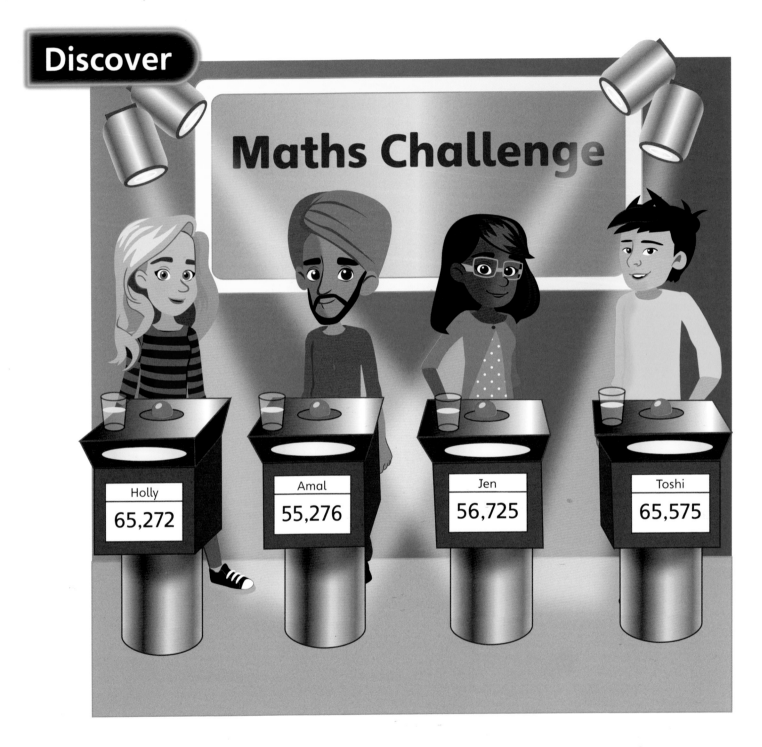

1 a) Who came first, with the highest score?

b) Write the scores in ascending order.

28

Share

a) All the scores are 5-digit numbers, so compare the digits with the highest place value first.

> I can see that two of the numbers only have 5 ten thousands, so I only need to compare the numbers with 6 ten thousands.

As the ten thousands digit is the same, compare the thousands digit.

Both numbers have 5 thousands, so compare the 100s.

65,272 only has 2 hundreds, whereas 65,575 has 5 hundreds.

TTh	Th	H	T	O
6	5	2	7	2
6	5	5	7	5

TTh	Th	H	T	O
6	5	2	7	2
6	5	5	7	5

65,575 is larger.   65,575 > 65,272

Toshi came first, with 65,575.

b) 55,276 and 56,725 both have the digit 5 in the ten thousands position so compare the 1,000s.

56,725 is larger than 55,276 because it has one more 1,000.

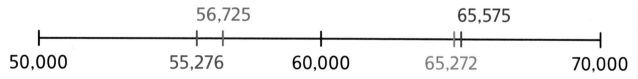

In ascending order, the scores are: 55,276, 56,725, 65,272, 65,575.

> Ascending means in order from lowest to highest.

Or 55,276 < 56,725 < 65,272 < 65,575

Think together

① Which bag of place value counters has the smaller total value?

A
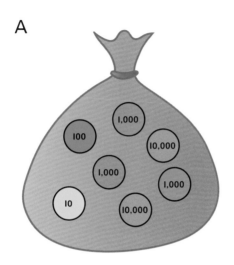

B
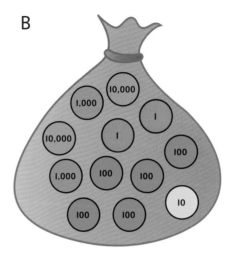

Bag ⬜ has a smaller value because ⬜ < ⬜.

② Which number in each pair is larger?

Use a place value grid to help make your decisions.

TTh	Th	H	T	O

a) 34,790 and 43,970

⬜ > ⬜

b) 21,033 and 8,968

⬜ > ⬜

3 Compare the numbers. Write them in descending order.

TTh	Th	H	T	O
2	0	9	2	3
	8	5	6	0
2	0	9	3	2

☐ > ☐ > ☐

4

A number starting with the digit 9 is larger than a number starting with the digit 5.

Reena

CHALLENGE

Is this statement always true, sometimes true or never true?

Prove your thinking in your own way.

I know! It is always true because 9 ten thousands is larger than 5 ten thousands.

I am not so sure. I think we need to think about this a little more.

→ **Practice book 5A p21**

Rounding numbers within 100,000

Discover

PALACE POOLS
Dive in at the deep end!

Rectangular pool

98,275 litres of water

Circular pool

41,300 litres of water

Oval pool

77,735 litres of water

1 **a)** For the rectangular pool, round the number of litres of water to the nearest 10,000 litres.

b) How many litres of water, to the nearest 100 litres, does the oval pool hold?

32

Share

a) The rectangular pool holds 98,275 litres.

I will start by showing the next and previous multiples of 10,000, but there isn't a 10,000s number after 90,000!

Yes, there is. 100,000 is also a multiple of 10,000. It is 10 groups of 10,000.

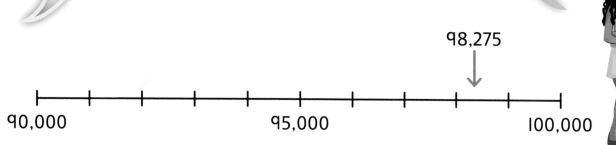

98,275

90,000   95,000   100,000

The number is closer to 100,000 than it is to 90,000.

98,275 litres rounds up to 100,000 litres to the nearest 10,000 litres.

To round to the nearest 10,000, look at the 1,000s digit and use the rules for rounding.

b) The oval pool holds 77,735 litres.

Check the 10s digit to round to the nearest 100.

77,735 has 3 tens so it rounds down to the previous multiple of 100.

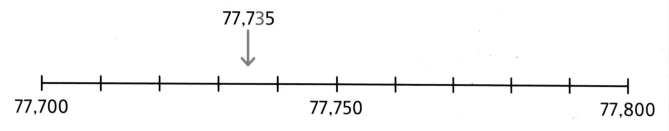

77,735

77,700   77,750   77,800

The oval pool holds 77,700 litres of water to the nearest 100 litres.

33

Think together

 a) For the circular pool, round the number of litres of water to the nearest 1,000 litres.

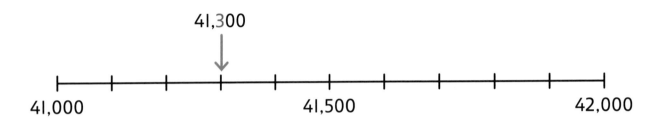

41,300

41,000   41,500   42,000

The circular pool holds 41,300 litres of water.

41,300 is between ☐,000 and ☐,000 on a number line.

41,300 is closer to ☐ .

41,300 litres rounds to ☐ litres to the nearest 1,000 litres.

b) Max rounds 41,300 to the nearest 10,000 without using a number line.

Which digit does Max need to look at?

Max needs to look at the ☐ digit.

c) Now round 41,300 to the nearest 10,000.

41,300 litres rounds to ☐ litres to the nearest 10,000 litres.

d) Complete the sentence.

77,735 litres rounded to the nearest ☐ litres is 77,740 litres.

2 Is Aki correct?

The number of litres in the rectangular pool rounds to 98,290 litres to the nearest 10.

Aki

Draw a number line and use this to explain your decision to your partner.

3 Jamilla sorts numbers into a table by using the rules for rounding.

CHALLENGE

I looked at the digits to help me to make a decision when rounding.

Jamilla

Rounds down to the previous 1,000	Rounds up to the next 1,000
44,412 53,045 34,615 1,499	26,322 39,785 85,488 5,259 78,901

Check Jamilla's rounding and correct any mistakes she has made.

Explain to your partner why you think she made these mistakes.

I wonder if Jamilla thought carefully about the digit that is important when rounding to the nearest 1,000.

35

→ Practice book 5A p24

Roman numerals to 10,000

Discover

1	I	11	XI	30	XXX
2	II	12	XII	40	XL
3	III	13	XIII	50	L
4	IV	14	XIV	60	LX
5	V	15	XV	70	LXX
6	VI	16	XVI	80	LXXX
7	VII	17	XVII	90	XC
8	VIII	18	XVIII	100	C
9	IX	19	XIX	500	D
10	X	20	XX	1,000	M

XXXIV

MDCXC   LXXV   MCDXX

Ebo   Jamie   Zac

1 **a)** What number do Ebo's Roman numerals represent?

b) Jamie wants to represent the number 74 in Roman numerals.

Which extra Roman numeral will she need to cut out?

Write 74 in Roman numerals.

Share

a) Ebo's Roman numerals are MDCXC.

XC means 100 – 10 = 90.

So MDCXC means 1,000 + 500 + 100 + 90.

M   D   C

We read Roman numerals from left to right. When there is a smaller number in front of a larger number, subtract the smaller number from the larger one.

Ebo's Roman numerals represent the number 1,690.

b) Jamie's Roman numerals are LXXV.

LXXV means 50 + 10 + 10 + 5 = 75

L   X   X   V

I can also say that XX means 20, so 50 + 20 + 5 = 75.

The number 74 is one less than 75. Jamie needs to subtract 1 from 5.

V means 5.

I means 1.

IV means 5 – 1 = 4.

Jamie needs to cut out the Roman numeral I and put it before the V.

74 in Roman numerals is LXXIV.

LXXIV

Think together

1 The part-whole model represents Zac's number in Roman numerals.

What is Zac's number?

M means ☐

CD means ☐ – ☐ = ☐

XX means ☐ + ☐ = ☐

☐ + ☐ + ☐ = ☐
M CD XX

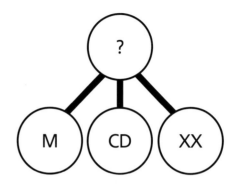

Zac's number is ☐ .

2 Complete the number sentences.

a)

XCVII means ☐ .

c)

MMIX means ☐ .

b)

450 means ☐ .

d)

1791 means ☐ .

3 What are the missing Roman numerals?

a) MC☐XX means 1,920.

b) DCC☐IV means 754.

c) ☐C☐X means 99.

4 Check the answers to Emma's calculations and correct any mistakes she has made.

CHALLENGE

I have made a page for my Roman project to show how to calculate using Roman numerals!

Emma

I think I will convert each calculation to numbers, work out the answer and then convert the answer back to Roman numerals.

ROMAN NUMERALS

a) MMD – C = MMCD

b) LVII + XXV = LXXVVII

c) MM ÷ X = MMX

d) M – CL = DCCCL

e) DXC + XVI = DCXXCI

39

End of unit check

1 What is the value of the 9 in the number 8,898?

A   9   B   90   C   900   D   9,000

2 Round 53,609 to the nearest 1,000.

A   53,000   B   52,000   C   50,000   D   54,000

3 Which number is represented on the place value grid?

TTh	Th	H	T	O
10,000 10,000 10,000 10,000 10,000 10,000 10,000 10,000	1,000 1,000 1,000 1,000		10 10 10	1 1 1 1 1 1

A   8,436   B   84,036   C   84,306   D   80,436

4 Which partitioning sentence is incorrect for the number 33,575?

A   33,575 = 20,000 + 13,000 + 500 + 75

B   33,575 = 20,000 + 10,000 + 500 + 70 + 5

C   33,575 = 30,000 + 2,000 + 1,500 + 70 + 5

D   33,575 = 30,000 + 3,000 + 500 + 70 + 5

5 Which number is a good estimate for the value of the triangle on this number line?

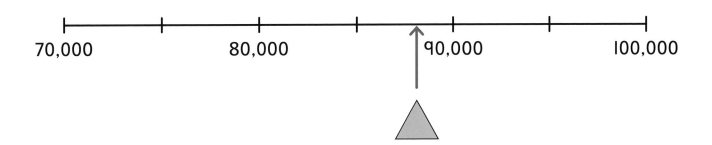

| A | 87,850 | | B | 85,320 | | C | 89,500 | | D | 84,625 |

6 These numbers are ordered from smallest to largest.

30,475   30,574   _____   31,000   31,095

Which is the missing number?

| A | 31,200 | | B | 3,065 | | C | 30,580 | | D | 31,011 |

7 Which number does not round to 20,000 to the nearest 10,000?

| A | 23,999 | | B | 14,870 | | C | 15,500 | | D | 20,009 |

8 Write the year 2019 in Roman numerals.

41

→ Practice book 5A p30

Unit 2
Place value within 1,000,000

In this unit we will ...

⚡ Understand the value of any digit in a number up to 1,000,000

⚡ Compare and order numbers to 1,000,000

⚡ Round numbers to the nearest 10, 100, 1,000, 10,000 and 100,000

⚡ Use negative numbers

⚡ Create number sequences

We need to be able to extend the place value grid to include millions.

M	HTh	TTh	Th	H	T	O

We will need some maths words. How many of these can you remember?

ones (1s)   tens (10s)   hundreds (100s)

thousands (1,000s)   ten thousands (10,000s)

hundred thousands (100,000s)   million (1,000,000)

round   order   ascending   descending

less than (<)   greater than (>)   sequence

We need to be able to use a number line and recognise where each number lies on a number line.

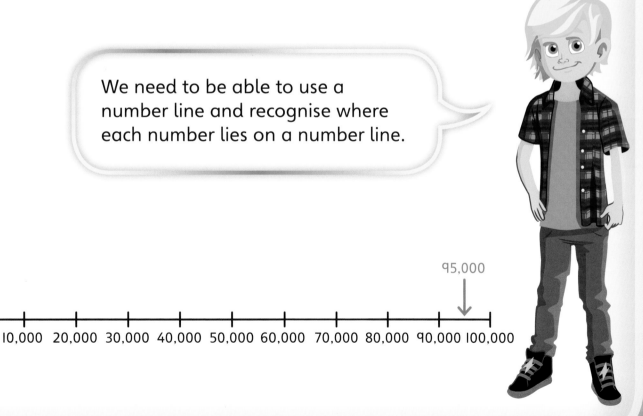

95,000

0   10,000   20,000   30,000   40,000   50,000   60,000   70,000   80,000   90,000   100,000

100,000s, 10,000s, 1,000s, 100s, 10s and 1s ①

Discover

Number of sweets made today: 461,905

Amal

Sofia

Contains 100,000 sweets

① a) How many sweets can six containers hold?

b) How many sweets have been made today? What does each digit in the number represent?

44

Share

a) Six containers can hold 600,000 sweets.

Each container holds 100,000 sweets. I will count up in 100,000s.

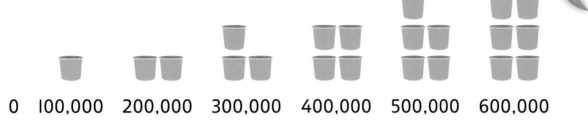

0   100,000   200,000   300,000   400,000   500,000   600,000

b) The board says that 461,905 sweets have been made today.

HTh	TTh	Th	H	T	O
100,000 100,000 100,000 100,000	10,000 10,000 10,000 10,000 10,000 10,000	1,000	100 100 100 100 100 100 100 100 100		1 1 1 1 1
4	6	1	9	0	5

There are 4 hundred thousands.

There are 6 ten thousands.

There is 1 thousand.

There are 9 hundreds.

There are 0 tens and 5 ones.

HTh in the place value grid means hundred thousands.

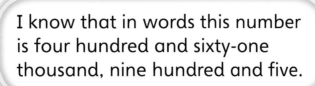

I know that in words this number is four hundred and sixty-one thousand, nine hundred and five.

45

Think together

1 How many sweets are shown here?

There are ☐ sweets.

2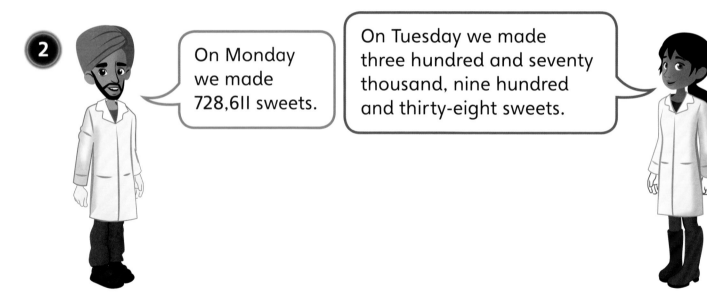

On Monday we made 728,611 sweets.

On Tuesday we made three hundred and seventy thousand, nine hundred and thirty-eight sweets.

a) Say out loud the number of sweets made on Monday. Now write it in words.

In words: _____

b) Write the number of sweets made on Tuesday in numerals.

In numerals: ☐

3 What does the digit 5 represent in each of these numbers?

CHALLENGE

a)

Three hundred and fifty-two thousand, nine hundred

Max

b)

128,745

Jamie

c)

HTh	TTh	Th	H	T	O
100,000 100,000	10,000		100 100 100 100 100	10 10	1 1 1 1 1 1
					1

d) 10,000 10,000 10,000   1,000 1,000 1,000 1,000 1,000   100 100   10 10 10 10 10   10 10 10

e)

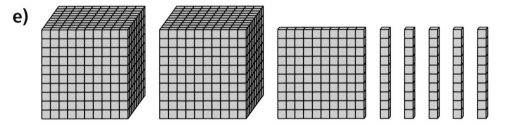

I do not think all of these numbers have 6 digits.

Make up your own number with 4, 5 or 6 digits. Ask your friend to read it aloud to you and represent it in different ways.

47

→ **Practice book 5A p32**

100,000s, 10,000s, 1,000s, 100s, 10s and 1s ②

Discover

1 **a)** How much money is in the bank vault? Write the answer in digits and words.

   b) Another vault has £360,400 in it. Find two ways that this could be made using the same types of sack as in the picture.

Share

I will use a place value grid to represent the amount of money in the bank vault.

a)

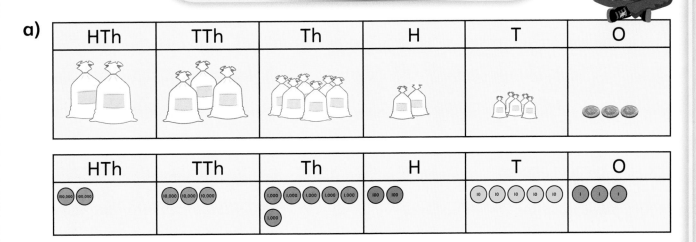

In digits: there is £236,253 in the bank vault.

In words: this is two hundred and thirty-six thousand, two hundred and fifty-three pounds.

b) There is £360,400 in the other bank vault.

HTh	TTh	Th	H	T	O

HTh	TTh	Th	H	T	O

There are three bags of £100,000, six bags of £10,000 and four bags of £100.

You could also have three bags of £100,000, five bags of £10,000, ten bags of £1,000 and four bags of £100.

I could exchange some of the bags. For example, I know that one bag of £10,000 is equal to ten bags of £1,000.

Think together

1 How much money is in each bank vault? Write your answers in digits and words.

a)

HTh	TTh	Th	H	T	O

In digits: there is £ ☐ in the bank vault.

In words: this is _____ .

b)

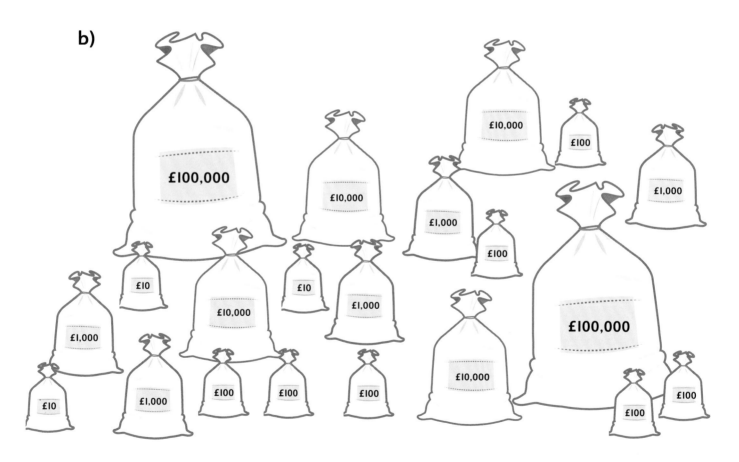

In digits: there is £ ☐ in the bank vault.

In words: this is _____ .

2 How many of each sack will you need to make £577,182?

 £100,000

 £10,000

 £1,000

 £100

 £10

You will need: _____ .

3 Complete the following partitions.

CHALLENGE

a) 726,140 is equal to ☐ hundred thousands,

☐ ten thousands, ☐ thousands, ☐ hundred and ☐ tens.

b) 58,415 is equal to ☐ ten thousands, ☐ thousands,

☐ hundreds, ☐ tens and ☐ ones.

c) 6 hundred thousands, 4 thousands and 2 hundreds = ☐

d) 951,618 = 900,000 + 50,000 + ☐,000 + ☐00 + ☐0 + ☐

e) 300,000 + 500 + 60 + 2 = ☐

I am going to use a place value grid to help me represent the numbers. This might help me partition them.

I wonder if there is another way I could partition the last number?

51

→ Practice book 5A p35

Number line to 1,000,000

Discover

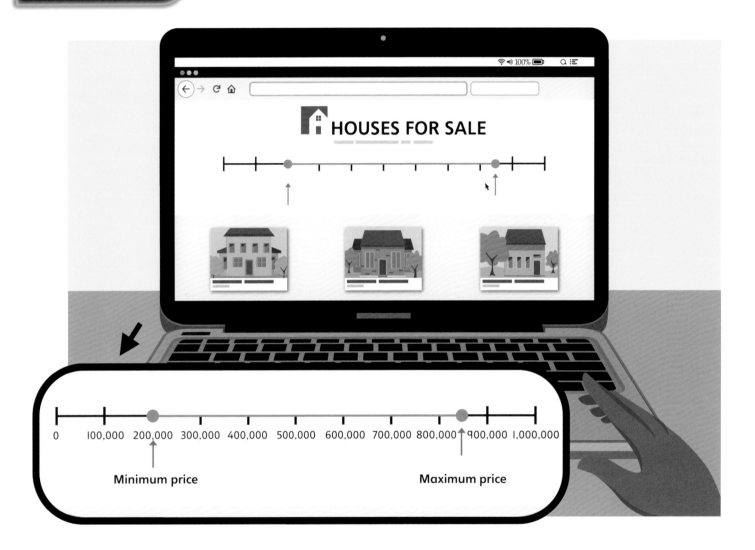

Minimum price

Maximum price

I a) Jen and Toshi are looking for a house to buy. What is the minimum and maximum price they search for on the website?

b) This house appears on their search.

Where would this house price appear on the number line?

£720,000

Share

> 1,000,000 is also known as one **million**.

a) The number line goes from 0 to 1,000,000.

There are 10 intervals.

The line goes up in intervals of 100,000s.

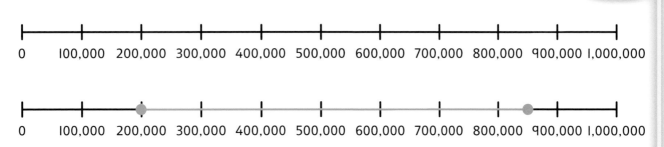

The minimum house price they search for on the website is £200,000.

The maximum house price is £850,000.

> The maximum house price lies half-way between 800,000 and 900,000.

b) The house costs £720,000.

£720,000 is greater than £700,000, but less than £800,000.

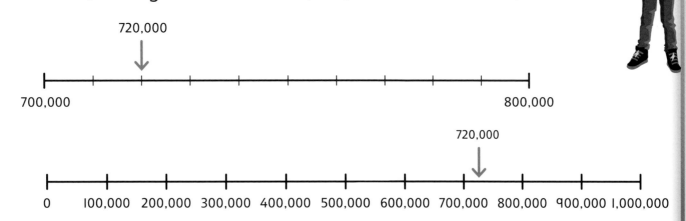

Think together

1 What are the missing numbers on each of these number lines?

a)

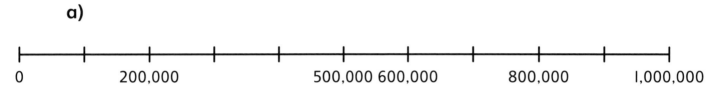

0   200,000   500,000 600,000   800,000   1,000,000

The missing numbers are: _____ .

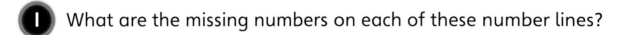

> Count aloud to check that you are going up by the correct amount each time.

b)

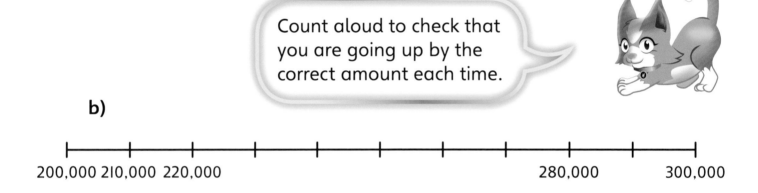

200,000 210,000 220,000   280,000   300,000

The missing numbers are: _____ .

c)

418,000   419,000

The missing numbers are: _____ .

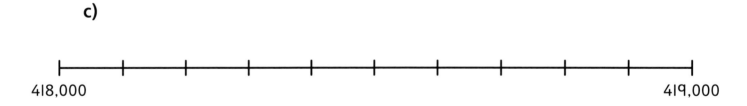

> I wonder, is there a way of working out what each line increases by?

2 What numbers are the arrows pointing to?

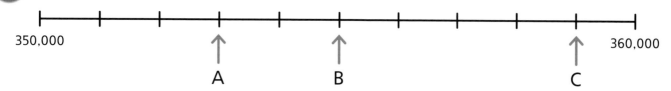

350,000   360,000

                    ↑   ↑   ↑
                    A   B   C

A = ☐   B = ☐   C = ☐

3 Jen and Toshi do a different search on the website and find these two houses.

£250,000   £295,000

Point to where each price would appear on each of these number lines.

a)

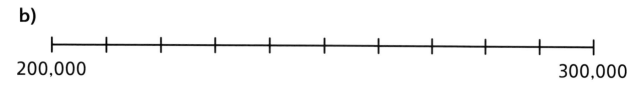

0   1,000,000

b)

200,000   300,000

c)

200,000   400,000

First, I need to work out what each line increases by.

55

Comparing and ordering numbers to 1,000,000

Discover

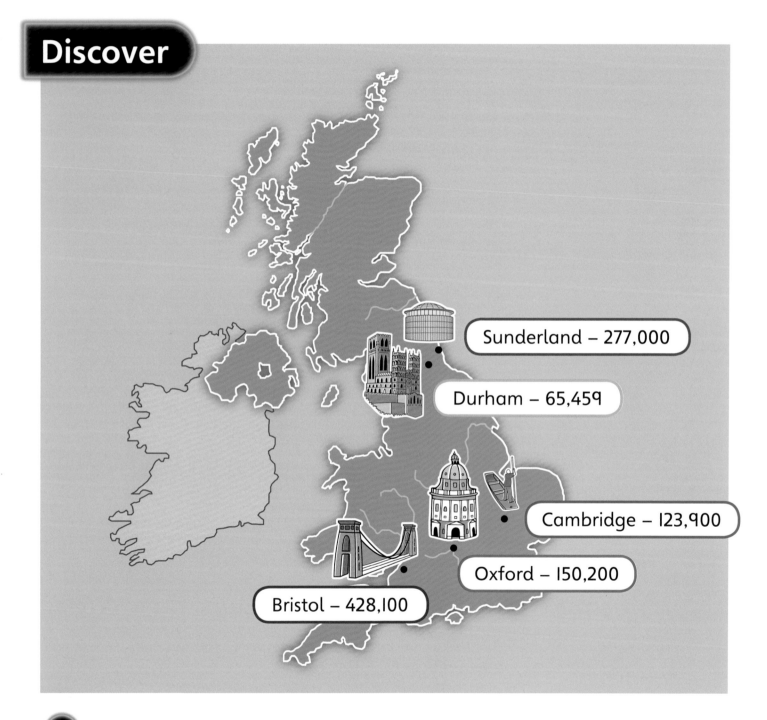

Sunderland – 277,000

Durham – 65,459

Cambridge – 123,900

Oxford – 150,200

Bristol – 428,100

1 **a)** Which has the greater population, Oxford or Cambridge?

b) Put the population of each city in ascending order.

Share

a) We compare the greatest place value first.

HTh	TTh	Th	H	T	O
1	5	0	2	0	0
1	2	3	9	0	0

Oxford
Cambridge

Both numbers have one 100,000. We now need to compare the 10,000s.

HTh	TTh	Th	H	T	O
1	5	0	2	0	0
1	2	3	9	0	0

Oxford
Cambridge

Oxford has more 10,000s so it has the greater population.

150,200 > 123,900

b)

I put the numbers in a place value grid. I compared the 100,000s first and then the 10,000s.

	HTh	TTh	Th	H	T	O
Durham		6	5	4	5	9
Cambridge	1	2	3	9	0	0
Oxford	1	5	0	2	0	0
Sunderland	2	7	7	0	0	0
Bristol	4	2	8	1	0	0

The populations in ascending order are Durham, Cambridge, Oxford, Sunderland and Bristol.

Think together

① Here are two towns in England.

Which of these towns has the smaller population?

 < ☐

_____ has the smaller population.

② This map shows the population of five places in Scotland.

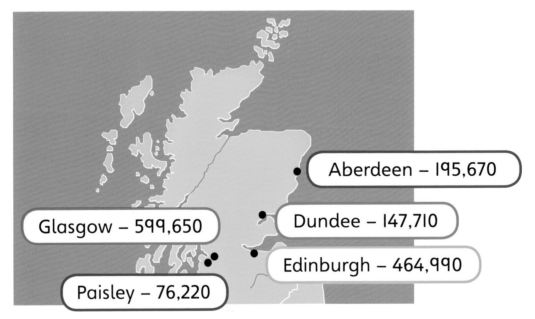

Which of these places has the third largest population?

_____ has the third largest population.

3 Which of these six numbers are less than three hundred and seventy-eight thousand?

195,311   four hundred thousand   99,999

308,000   seventy-nine thousand, two hundred   382,900

4 The following number cards are in ascending order.

What could the missing digits be?

72,500

126,☐91

12☐,470

1☐3,904

133,☐☐2

First, I will look at the 10,000s for each number.

I wonder if there is more than one possible digit for each space.

59

Rounding numbers to 1,000,000

Discover

My number rounds to 50,000 to the nearest 10,000.

Jamie

Danny

1 2 4 5 7 8

1 **a)** Danny makes the number 712,458 from the digit cards on the desk.

Round the number to the nearest 100,000.

Round the number to the nearest 100.

b) Jamie has used the digit cards to make a 5-digit number.

What number could Jamie have made?

Share

I looked at the size of the digits to help me round the numbers.

a) To round the 100,000s digit you look at the 10,000s digit.

HTh	TTh	Th	H	T	O
7	1	2	4	5	8

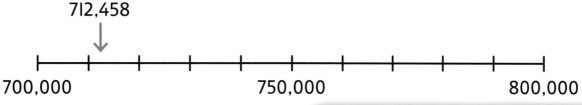

712,458

700,000   750,000   800,000

712,458 rounded to the nearest 100,000 is 700,000.

I used a number line to help me work out which 100,000 it is closer to.

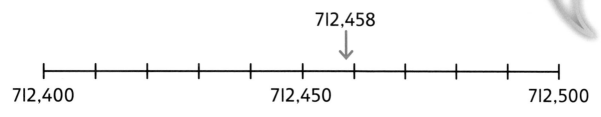

712,458

712,400   712,450   712,500

712,458 lies between 712,400 and 712,500.

712,458 lies closer to 712,500.

712,458 rounded to the nearest 100 is 712,500.

b) Jamie's number must lie between 45,000 and 54,999. All of the numbers in between will round to 50,000.

Here are some numbers that Jamie could have made.

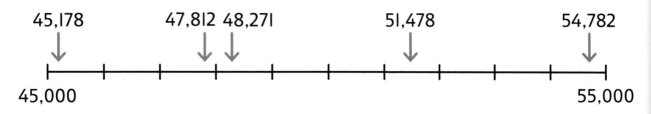

45,178   47,812 48,271   51,478   54,782

45,000   55,000

Think together

1 Jamie now makes this number.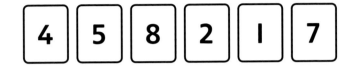

a) Round the number to the nearest 100,000.

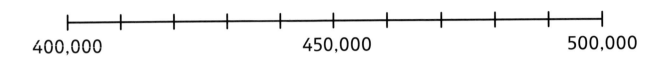

400,000   450,000   500,000

458,217 rounded to the nearest 100,000 is ☐ .

b) Round the number to the nearest 1,000.

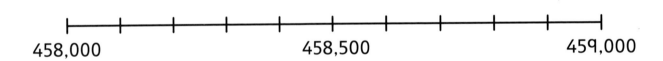

458,000   458,500   459,000

458,217 rounded to the nearest 1,000 is ☐ .

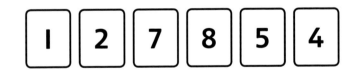

2 Danny makes this number.

What numbers should go into the table?

Danny's number, rounded to the nearest ...				
100,000	10,000	1,000	100	10

3 Danny and Jamie each have ten digit cards.

| 0 | 1 | 2 | 3 | 4 | 5 | 6 | 7 | 8 | 9 |

a) Danny makes this number.

| 9 | 1 | | 7 | | 2 |

Danny's number rounded to the nearest 1,000 is 916,000.

What could the missing digits be?

b) Jamie makes **two** 4-digit numbers from the same cards.

| 0 | 1 | 2 | 3 | 4 | 5 | 6 | 7 | 8 | 9 |

Both of Jamie's numbers rounded to the nearest 100 are 7,000.

Write two 4-digit numbers Jamie could have made.

I will use trial and error and then check after each guess.

I wonder how many different answers I can find to these questions.

63

→ Practice book 5A p44

Negative numbers

Discover

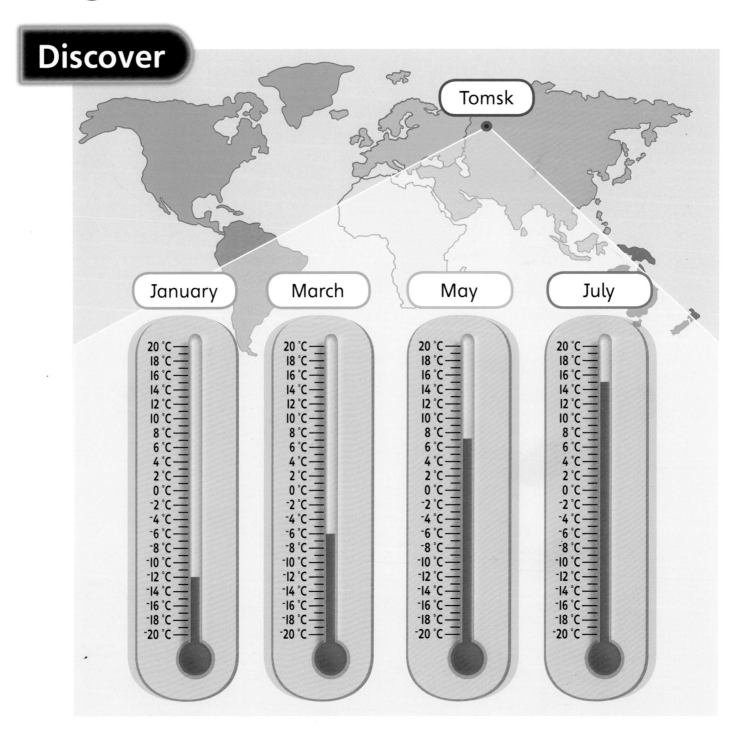

1 **a)** In Tomsk, how much warmer is May than March?

b) Which two months have the greatest difference in temperature?

What is the greatest difference?

Share

a) The temperature in March is ⁻6 °C.

The temperature in May is 7 °C.

I used a number line and counted how many degrees warmer it was. First I counted to 0, then on to 7.

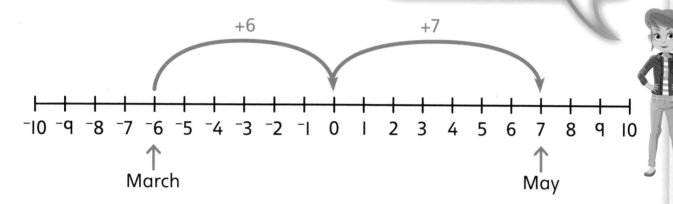

In Tomsk, May is 13 °C warmer than March.

b) The two months that have the greatest temperature difference are January and July.

January has the coldest temperature and July has the warmest.

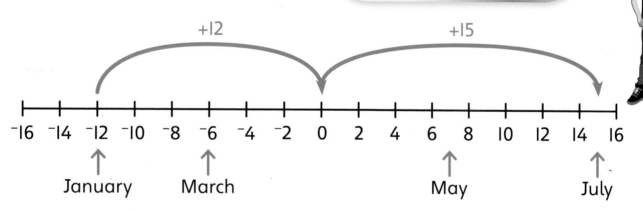

The difference in temperature between January and July is 27 °C.

The difference between ⁻12 and 0 is 12 °C.
The difference between 0 and 15 is 15 °C.
I added 12 and 15 to get 27 °C.

Think together

1 The table shows the temperatures in New York and Cairo.

New York	Cairo
⁻12 °C	9 °C

How much warmer is the temperature in Cairo than in New York?

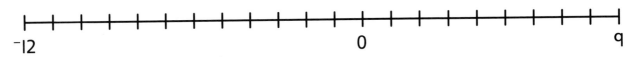

⁻12   0   9

Cairo is ⬜ °C warmer than New York.

2 A hotel has floors above and below ground.

Mrs Dean gets into the lift on floor 14.

She travels to the underground car park on floor ⁻5.

How many floors does she travel down?

⬜ floors

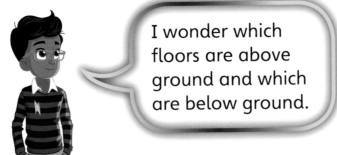

I wonder which floors are above ground and which are below ground.

66

3 The thermometers show the temperatures at different times of the day in a city.

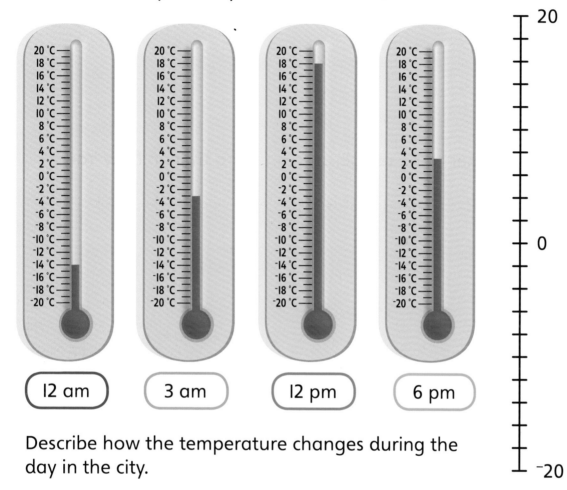

Describe how the temperature changes during the day in the city.

I will talk about how much it increases and decreases. I will use the number line to help me.

I might turn it into a weather report and present it to my friends.

67

Counting in 10s, 100s, 1,000s, 10,000s

Discover

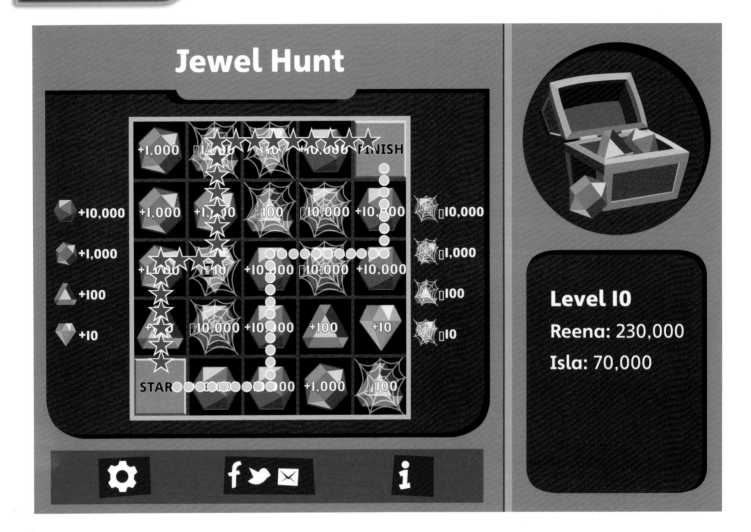

1 **a)** Isla and Reena are playing Jewel Hunt.

Isla starts on 70,000 points. She takes the dotted path.

Now follow the dotted path through the grid.

What is the score when Isla reaches the finish?

b) Reena takes the star path. She starts on 230,000 points.

What score does Reena have when she reaches the finish?

Share

a) Isla starts with 70,000 points.

I noticed that I was counting up and down in 10,000s.

80,000 | 90,000 | 100,000 | 110,000 | 120,000 | 110,000 | 120,000

When Isla reaches the finish her score is 120,000.

b) Reena starts with 230,000 points.

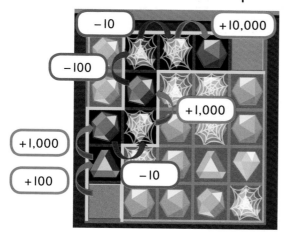

I made 230,000 from counters and added and removed counters as I went. Sometimes I had to exchange.

230,100 | 231,100 | 231,090 | 232,090 | 231,990 | 231,980 | 241,980

When Reena reaches the finish her score is 241,980.

69

Think together

1 Work out the missing numbers in each sequence.

a) 72,000 , 73,000 , 74,000 , [ ] , [ ] , [ ]

b) 272,800 , 272,900 , [ ] , [ ] , 273,200 , [ ]

c) 738,006 , [ ] , [ ] , 438,006 , [ ] , [ ]

2 Use the place value grid to complete the table below.

HTh	TTh	Th	H	T	O
1	4	7	3	0	0

100,000 less		100,000 more	
10,000 less		10,000 more	
1,000 less		1,000 more	
100 less		100 more	
10 less		10 more	

3 Isla and Reena are now on a different level of Jewel Hunt.

a) Reena starts with 400,500 points. She takes this path.

What score does Reena have by the end of the level?

What do you notice?

b) Isla starts with 500,000 points.

What path could Isla take through the maze to finish with less than 500,000 points?

I will use trial and error and do it in my head.

I am going to look at the maze first and see if I notice anything.

71

Number sequences

Discover

1 **a)** How many tiles will Olivia and Ebo need to make pattern number 5?

b) Another pattern has 42 tiles. Which pattern number is this?

Share

a)

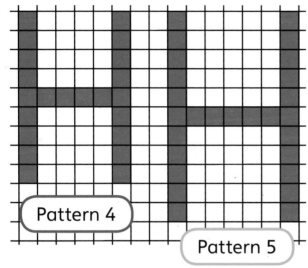

Pattern 4

Pattern 5

I drew pattern 4 and pattern 5.

Olivia and Ebo will need 27 tiles to make pattern number 5.

b)

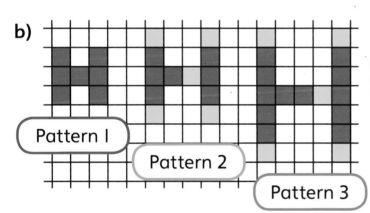

Pattern 1

Pattern 2

Pattern 3

I noticed that the number of tiles increased by 5 each time. I kept adding on 5 until I got to 42.

Pattern	1	2	3	4	5	6	7	8
Number of tiles	7	12	17	22	27	32	37	42

Pattern 8

Pattern number 8 has 42 tiles.

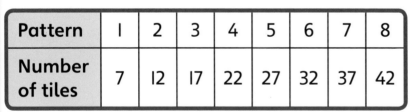

73

Think together

1 Here are some different tiling patterns.

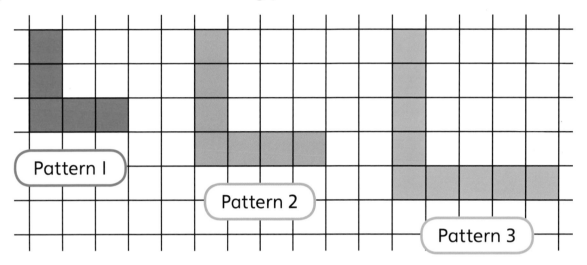

Pattern 1

Pattern 2

Pattern 3

a) How many tiles are needed to make pattern number 5?

b) Which pattern needs 15 tiles? Complete the table to help you.

Pattern	1	2	3	4	5			
Number of tiles								

2 What are the next three numbers in each of these sequences?

a) 6, 10, 14, ☐ , ☐ , ☐

b) 23, 26, 29, 32, ☐ , ☐ , ☐

c) 800, 750, 700, 650, ☐ , ☐ , ☐

d) 10, 7, 4, ☐ , ☐ , ☐

e) ⁻11, ⁻7, ⁻3, ☐ , ☐ , ☐

Describe the pattern in each sequence.

3 Look at this sequence of tiling patterns.

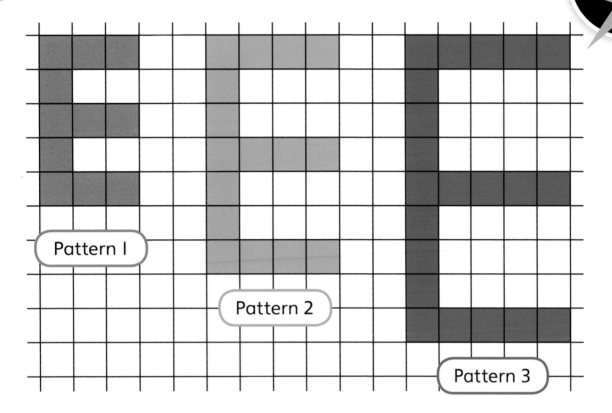

Pattern 1

Pattern 2

Pattern 3

CHALLENGE

Which number pattern will be the first to have more than 50 tiles?

I am going to make a table of results and see if I can find a pattern.

I wonder if there are any other letters that I can make with tiles to form a pattern.

→ **Practice book 5A p53**

End of unit check

1 In the number 218,705, what does the digit 8 represent?

A 80,000   B 8,000   C 800   D 80

2 What is seven hundred thousand and thirty-five in numerals?

A 70,035   B 700,350   C 700,035   D 735

3 What is the missing number?

356,405 = 300,000 + 50,000 + 6,000 + ☐ + 5

A 4   B 40   C 400   D 4,000

4 What is the missing number?

| 166,230 | 176,230 | 186,230 | 196,230 | ☐ | 216,230 |

A 296,230   B 197,230   C 206,230   D 196,231

5 What number is the arrow pointing to?

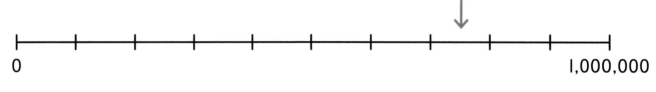

A 7.5   B 75   C 75,000   D 750,000

6 Reena is thinking of a number.

My number is even.

My number rounds to 67,000 to the nearest 1,000.

Reena

What is the greatest even number Reena could be thinking about?

7 The thermometers show the temperature at 12 noon and 12 midnight in a town.

What is the difference in temperature between noon and midnight?

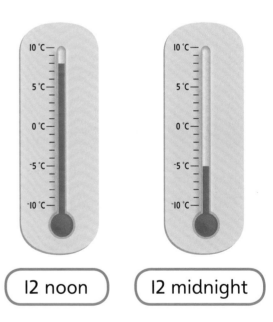

12 noon   12 midnight

77

→ Practice book 5A p56

Unit 3
Addition and subtraction

In this unit we will …

- ⚡ Add and subtract numbers with up to 5 digits
- ⚡ Use the column method for addition and subtraction
- ⚡ Round numbers to estimate answers to problems
- ⚡ Add and subtract mentally
- ⚡ Solve problems involving addition and subtraction

What information does this comparison bar model give you? What can you use it to work out?

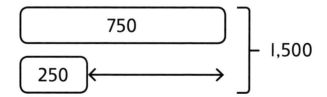

750

1,500

250

We will need some maths words.
How many of these can you remember?

add   subtract   ones (1s)   tens (10s)

hundreds (100s)   thousands (1,000s)

ten thousands (10,000s)   mentally

inverse   round   estimate

distance chart

Laying a calculation out neatly in
columns can help us to understand
the value of each digit.

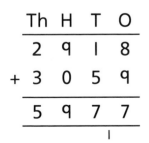

	Th	H	T	O
	2	9	1	8
+	3	0	5	9
	5	9	7	7
			1	

Th	H	T	O
1,000 1,000	100 100 100 100 100 / 100 100 100 100	10	1 1 1 1 1 1 / 1 1 1
1,000 1,000 1,000		10 10 10 10 10 10	1 1 1 1 1 1 / 1 1 1 1

Adding whole numbers with more than 4 digits ①

Discover

Day	Number of views
Monday	21,630
Tuesday	20,153
Wednesday	19,175
Thursday	22,571
Friday	18,417

① a) What is the total number of video views for Tuesday and Wednesday?

b) Which two days have the total number of views of 37,592?

Share

a) Add the number of video views for Tuesday and Wednesday.

> I will use counters to help me.
>
> I will set out the work in columns and add them together, starting with the smallest place value.

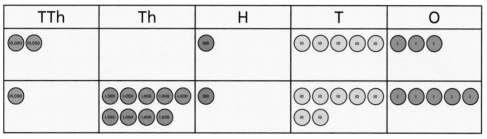

TTh	Th	H	T	O

TTh	Th	H	T	O
2	0	1	5	3
+ 1	9	1	7	5
3	9	3	2	8

The total number of video views for Tuesday and Wednesday is 39,328.

b)

	TTh	Th	H	T	O
Monday	2	1	6	3	0
Tuesday +	2	0	1	5	3
	4	1	7	8	3

	TTh	Th	H	T	O
Monday	2	1	6	3	0
Wednesday +	1	9	1	7	5
	4	0	8	0	5

	TTh	Th	H	T	O
Wednesday	1	9	1	7	5
Friday +	1	8	4	1	7
	3	7	5	9	2

> I will use trial and improvement to find the correct 2 days.
>
> I will need to take my time and be careful not to miss any.

The last digit of Wednesday is 5.

The last digit of Friday is 7.

$5 + 7 = 12$

> I think there may be a way you can tell by just adding the last digits.

Wednesday and Friday have the total number of views of 37,592.

Think together

1 What is the total number of views for Thursday and Friday?

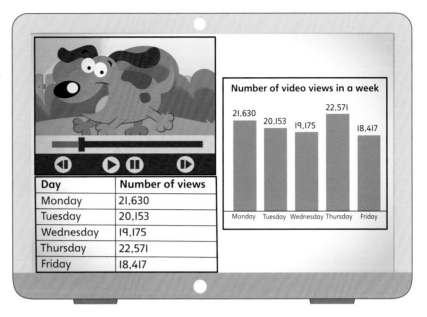

Day	Number of views
Monday	21,630
Tuesday	20,153
Wednesday	19,175
Thursday	22,571
Friday	18,417

Number of video views in a week

TTh	Th	H	T	O

	TTh	Th	H	T	O
	2	2	5	7	1
+	1	8	4	1	7

The total number of views is ⬚ .

2 On Saturday, the video is viewed 1,564 times. What is the total number of views for Friday and Saturday?

TTh	Th	H	T	O

	TTh	Th	H	T	O
		1	5	6	4
+	1	8	4	1	7

The total number of views is ⬚ .

82

3 Here are the total views for four other videos.

Work out the total views for any two of the videos.

Then see if your partner can work out which two videos you added together.

The last digits will help me work out which two videos my partner added.

Be careful when the numbers do not have the same number of digits. Remember to set out the addition correctly.

83

→ **Practice book 5A p58**

Adding whole numbers with more than 4 digits 2

Discover

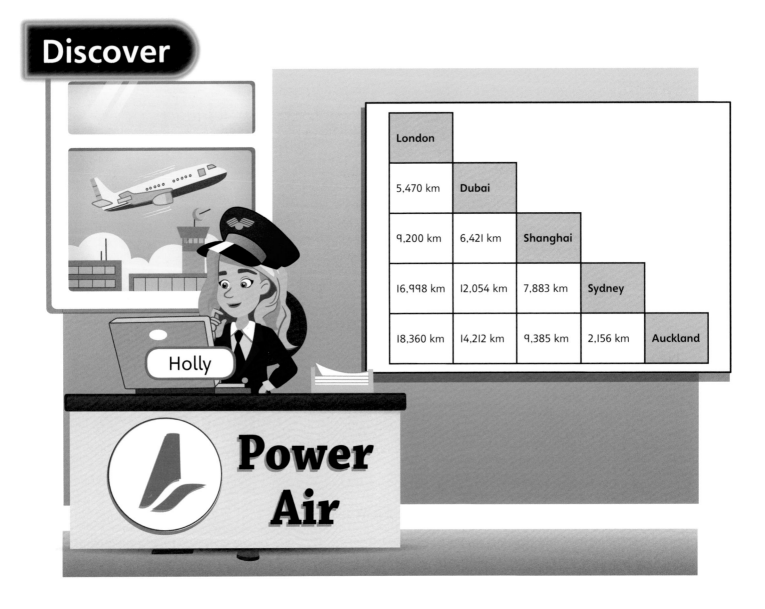

London				
5,470 km	Dubai			
9,200 km	6,421 km	Shanghai		
16,998 km	12,054 km	7,883 km	Sydney	
18,360 km	14,212 km	9,385 km	2,156 km	Auckland

1 **a)** What is the distance between London and Sydney?

Which two cities are 9,385 km apart?

b) Holly flies from London to Auckland and then from Auckland to Dubai.

How many km does Holly fly in total?

Share

a) Look down the column for London until you get to the row for Sydney.

This is the distance between the two cities.

> This is called a **distance chart** or table. It tells you the distances between two places.

London				
5,470 km	Dubai			
9,200 km	6,421 km	Shanghai		
16,998 km	12,054 km	7,883 km	Sydney	
18,360 km	14,212 km	9,385 km	2,156 km	Auckland

The distance between London and Sydney is 16,998 km.

Next, find 9,385 km in the table.

It is in the column that says Shanghai.

Shanghai		
7,883 km	Sydney	
9,385 km	2,156 km	Auckland

It is in the row that says Auckland.

Shanghai and Auckland are 9,385 km apart.

b) The distance from London to Auckland is 18,360 km.

The distance from Auckland to Dubai is 14,212 km.

```
TTh Th  H  T  O
  1  8  3  6  0
+ 1  4  2  1  2
  3  2  5  7  2
     1
```

> I used the chart to find the distances that I needed to add together. Then I used a column method to add the numbers.

Holly flies 32,572 km in total.

Think together

1 Mo flies from London to Sydney. He then flies from Sydney to Auckland.

London				
5,470 km	Dubai			
9,200 km	6,421 km	Shanghai		
16,998 km	12,054 km	7,883 km	Sydney	
18,360 km	14,212 km	9,385 km	2,156 km	Auckland

How many km does Mo fly in total?

Mo flies ⬚ km in total.

```
  TTh Th  H  T  O
    1  6  9  9  8
 +     2  1  5  6
  ───────────────

  ───────────────
```

2 David wants to fly to Auckland.

There are two possible routes that he can take.

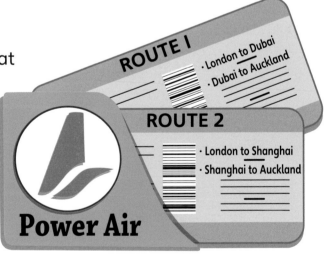

ROUTE I
· London to Dubai
· Dubai to Auckland

ROUTE 2
· London to Shanghai
· Shanghai to Auckland

Power Air

Which route should David choose if he wants to travel the shortest distance?

David should choose _____ .

3 Ebo is on a round the world trip.

He travels from Dubai to Shanghai to Auckland, and then to London.

London				
5,470 km	**Dubai**			
9,200 km	6,421 km	**Shanghai**		
16,998 km	12,054 km	7,883 km	**Sydney**	
18,360 km	14,212 km	9,385 km	2,156 km	**Auckland**

a) How far does he travel in total?

Ebo travels ☐ km in total.

b) Look at how Dexter and Flo answered the question.
Do both methods give the same answer?

I am going to add all three distances together at the same time.

I think I will get the same answer if I add the first two distances, and then add on the final distance.

c) Which method do you prefer?

→ Practice book 5A p61

Subtracting whole numbers with more than 4 digits ❶

Discover

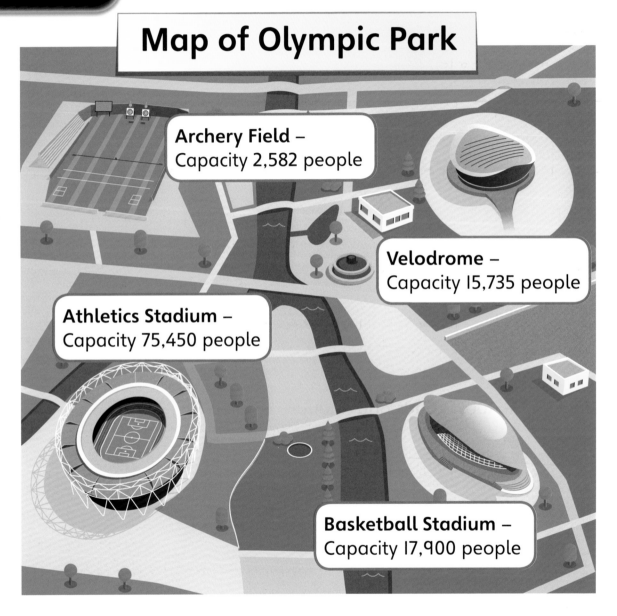

Map of Olympic Park

Archery Field – Capacity 2,582 people

Velodrome – Capacity 15,735 people

Athletics Stadium – Capacity 75,450 people

Basketball Stadium – Capacity 17,900 people

❶ **a)** How much greater is the capacity of the velodrome than the capacity of the archery field?

b) On the first day there were 52,700 people in the athletics stadium.

How many seats were empty?

Share

a) The capacity of the velodrome is 15,735 people.

The capacity of the archery field is 2,582 people.

First subtract the 1s.

To find out how many more, I need to do a subtraction.

TTh	Th	H	T	O
●	●●●●●	●●●●● ●●● ●●	●●●	●●●⊘⊘

TTh	Th	H	T	O
1	5	7	3	5
−		2	5	8	2
				3

Now subtract the 10s. Exchange 1 hundred for 10 tens.

TTh	Th	H	T	O
●	●●●●●	●●●●● ●⊘	●●●●● ⊘⊘⊘⊘⊘ ⊘⊘⊘	●●●⊘⊘

TTh	Th	H	T	O
1	5	⁶7̶	¹3	5
−		2	5	8	2
			5	3

Subtract the 100s, 1,000s and 10,000s.

TTh	Th	H	T	O
●	●●●⊘⊘	●●⊘⊘⊘ ⊘⊘⊘	●●●●● ⊘⊘⊘⊘⊘ ⊘⊘⊘	●●●⊘⊘

TTh	Th	H	T	O
1	5	⁶7̶	¹3	5
−		2	5	8	2
1	3	1	5	3

The velodrome capacity is 13,153 greater than the archery field capacity.

b)

75,450	
52,700	?

22,750 seats were empty in the athletics stadium.

TTh	Th	H	T	O
7	⁴8̶	¹4	5	0
− 5	2	7	0	0
2	2	7	5	0

Think together

Velodrome –
Capacity 15,735 people

1 The velodrome is full. At 2 pm, 3,620 people leave.

How many people are left in the velodrome?

TTh	Th	H	T	O
●	●●●●●	●●●●●●● ●●	●●●	●●●●●

TTh	Th	H	T	O
1	5	7	3	5
−	3	6	2	0

There are ⬜ people left in the velodrome.

2 There are 10,840 people watching a game at the basketball stadium.

How many more people could have watched the game?

17,900	
10,840	?

TTh	Th	H	T	O
1	7	9	0	0
− 1	0	8	4	0

⬜ more people could have watched the game.

3 The capacity of the hockey centre is 42,300 less than the capacity of the athletics stadium.

| **Athletics Stadium –** Capacity 75,450 people | **Velodrome –** Capacity 15,735 people | **Hockey Centre –** Capacity ? |

How much greater is the capacity of the hockey centre than the capacity of the velodrome?

Athletics Stadium | 75,450

Hockey Centre | ⟵———⟶ 42,300

Velodrome | 15,735 ⟵——⟶ ?

The capacity of the hockey centre is ☐ greater than the capacity of the velodrome.

First, I will find the capacity of the hockey centre by subtracting.

I think the bar model will help me work out how to find the difference.

→ Practice book 5A p64

Subtracting whole numbers with more than 4 digits ❷

Discover

Use all ten of the digit cards to make a subtraction with no exchanges.

There is no exchange needed.

Mr Lopez

Jamilla

Max

6 8 5 9 7
− 1 2 0 3 4

1 a) If you swap the 2 and the 8 cards, how many exchanges are needed now? What is the answer to the new subtraction?

b) Jamilla and Max swap some more of the cards.

Work out the answers to each of these subtractions.

TTh	Th	H	T	O
6	2	0	9	7
− 1	8	5	3	4

TTh	Th	H	T	O
6	2	0	3	7
− 1	8	5	9	4

TTh	Th	H	T	O
6	2	0	3	4
− 1	8	5	9	7

Share

a) When the 2 and 8 cards are swapped the subtraction looks like this:

```
TTh Th  H   T   O
 ⁵8̸ ¹2   5   9   7
-  1   8   0   3   4
_____
   4   4   5   6   3
```

I did a column subtraction like the ones in the last lesson.

One exchange is needed now, as there are not enough thousands to subtract from.

The answer to the new subtraction is 44,563.

b) The answers are as follows:

```
TTh Th  H   T   O
 ⁵8̸ ¹¹2̸ ¹0   9   7
-  1   8   5   3   4
_____
   4   3   5   6   3
```

```
TTh Th  H   T   O
 ⁵8̸ ¹¹2̸ ⁹10̸ ¹3   7
-  1   8   5   9   4
_____
   4   3   4   4   3
```

```
TTh Th  H   T   O
 ⁵8̸ ¹¹2̸ ⁹10̸ ¹²3̸ ¹4
-  1   8   5   9   7
_____
   4   3   4   3   7
```

Be careful not to subtract the digits in the number on the top line from the digits in the number on the bottom line.

In the last one, I will need to make an exchange in every column to make sure each number is big enough to subtract from.

Think together

1 Mr Lopez rearranges the cards again.

Work out the answer to this new subtraction.

    8 2 7 0 6

     − 3 9 4 1 5

TTh	Th	H	T	O
8	2	7	0	6
− 3	9	4	1	5

2 Mr Lopez arranges the digit cards into a new subtraction that the children complete. He has missed out some of the cards, as shown below:

1 2 6 8 9

Where do the missing digit cards go in the calculation?

    7 ☐ 5 0 3

     − ☐ 4 ☐ ☐ ☐

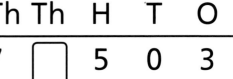

TTh	Th	H	T	O
7	☐	5	0	3
− ☐	4	☐	☐	☐
6	1	6	1	1

3 Use column subtraction to solve the following calculations.

CHALLENGE

a) 27,910 – 15,462

b) 27,900 – 15,462

c) 27,000 – 15,462

d) 20,000 – 15,462

What do you notice?

I have seen this method before. 4000 – 1278 is the same as 3999 – 1277.

There are a lot of exchanges. I wonder if there is a quicker method I could use. I could try subtracting one from each number.

→ **Practice book 5A p67**

Using rounding to estimate and check answers

Discover

1 **a)** How could Bella use rounding to check her answer?

What should the answer be close to?

b) What mistake has Bella made?

What is the correct answer?

Share

a)

4,012   17,877

0   2,000   4,000   6,000   8,000   10,000   12,000   14,000   16,000   18,000   20,000

Bella could round up both numbers
to the nearest thousand and add them.

I worked out what the
numbers were close to and
then added them together.

17,877 is close to 18,000.

4,012 is close to 4,000.

18,000 + 4,000 = 22,000

Bella's answer should be close to 22,000.

b) Bella has lined up the numbers incorrectly in the column addition.

The thousands need to be lined up underneath the thousands,
and so on.

Bella's working

TTh	Th	H	T	O
1	7	8	7	7
+ 4	0	1	2	
5	7	9	9	7

Correct method

TTh	Th	H	T	O
	1	7	8	7	7
+		4	0	1	2
	2	1	8	8	9
		1			

21,889 is close to 22,000 so the estimate was sensible.

The correct answer is 21,889.

Think together

1 Bella works on the next question.

Use rounding to show that Bella's answer must be incorrect.

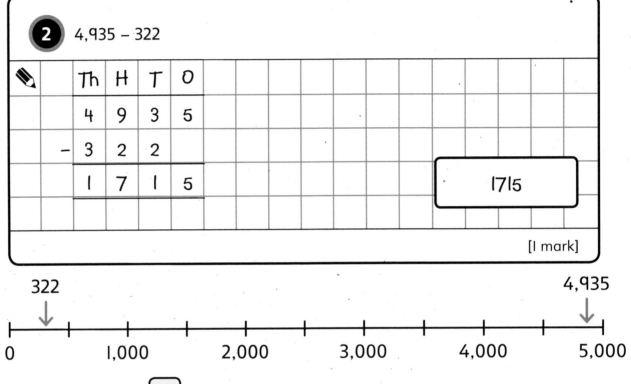

2 4,935 − 322

		Th	H	T	O
		4	9	3	5
	−	3	2	2	
		1	7	1	5

1715

[1 mark]

4,935 is close to ☐ .

322 is close to ☐ .

☐ − ☐ = ☐

What mistake has Bella made?

2 Use rounding to estimate the answer to the following calculations.

a) 17,240 + 28,385

b) 7,010 − 3,997

Now work out the answers to each of the questions.

Were your estimates sensible?

3

CHALLENGE

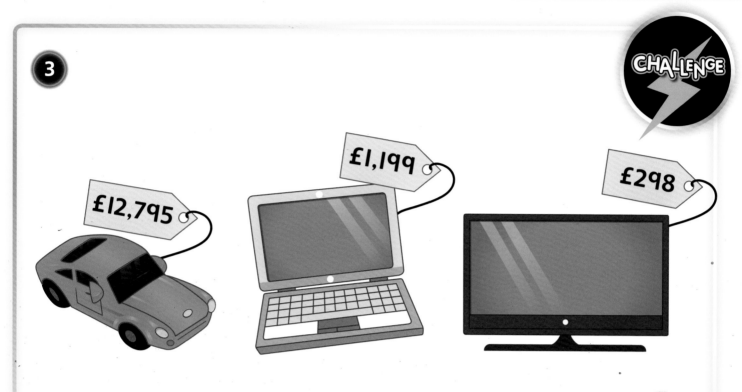

£12,795

£1,199

£298

a) How much do all of the items cost in total?

b) What is the difference in price between the car and the laptop?

I wonder if there are different strategies I could use to work out the answers.

I will use estimates to check if my answers are reasonable. I think there might be different estimates I could use.

99

→ Practice book 5A p70

Mental addition and subtraction ❶

Discover

❶ a) Work out the answers to Pair A in your head.

Now explain to your partner how you worked them out.

b) Work out the answers to Pair B in your head.

Now explain to your partner how you worked them out.

Share

In my head I worked out how many I need to add on to make the next 10, and then how many tens I need to add on.

a)

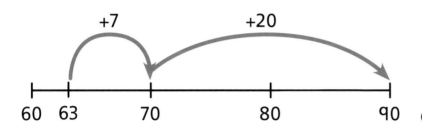

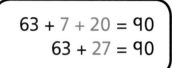

$$63 + 7 + 20 = 90$$
$$63 + 27 = 90$$

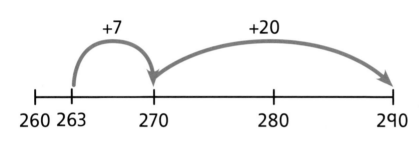

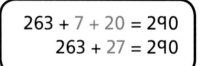

$$263 + 7 + 20 = 290$$
$$263 + 27 = 290$$

b) 45 + 23 =

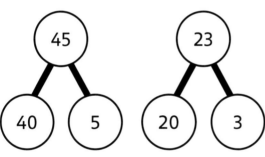

450 + 230 =

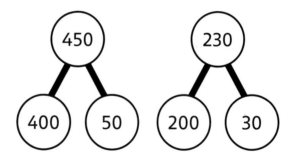

$$40 + 20 = 60$$
$$5 + 3 = 8$$
$$45 + 23 = 60 + 8 = 68$$

$$400 + 200 = 600$$
$$50 + 30 = 80$$
$$450 + 230 = 600 + 80 = 680$$

For these I looked at the parts and then added them separately. Finally, I added my answers at the end.

Think together

1   Work out the answers to the following questions in your head.

Explain your method to your partner.

a) 47 + 35

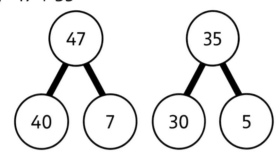

b) 350 + 470

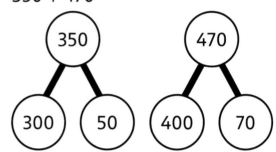

40 + 30 = ☐

7 + 5 = ☐

47 + 35 = ☐ + ☐ = ☐

300 + 400 = ☐

50 + 70 = ☐

350 + 470 = ☐ + ☐ = ☐

2   Work out the answers to these questions in your head.

Explain your method to your partner.

a)

74 + 69 = ☐

b)

740 + 690 = ☐

I added on 60 to 74 and then added on 9.

3 Andy is trying to work out the answers to the following calculations in his head.

$$324 + 198 = \boxed{}$$

$$324 + 197 = \boxed{}$$

Andy

I will first add 200 to 324

a) What does Andy need to do next to find the answer to each calculation?

b) Work out the answers to these calculations in your head.

$$672 + 99 = \boxed{}$$

$$7{,}608 + 1{,}998 = \boxed{}$$

$$426 + 397 = \boxed{}$$

$$18{,}790 + 39{,}990 = \boxed{}$$

$$296 + 3{,}147 = \boxed{}$$

I will add on more than I need to, and then subtract.

But how will you work out what to add on?

103

Mental addition and subtraction ❷

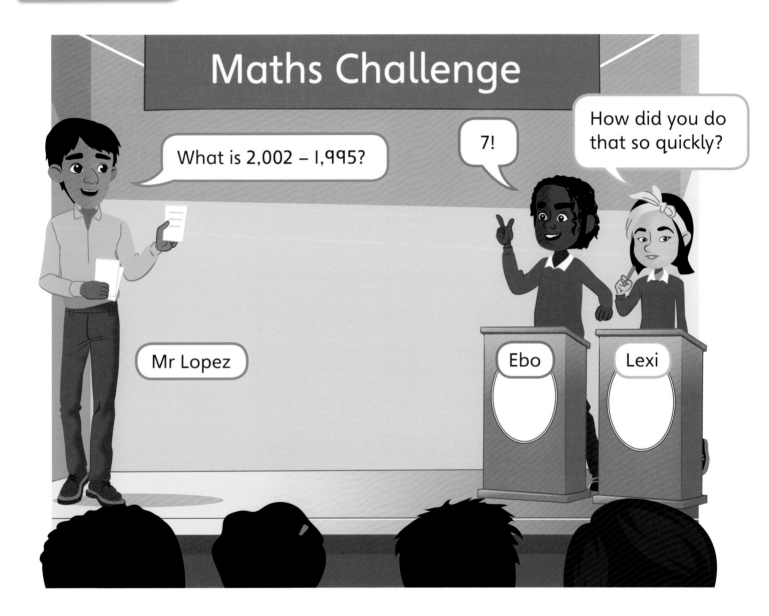

1 **a)** Explain how Ebo could have found the answer so quickly in his head.

b) Mr Lopez then asks, 'What is 760 – 250?'

Work out the answer mentally and explain your method to a partner.

Share

a)

These numbers are very close together.

I imagined a number line in my head and worked out how many I needed to count on.

$+5$ $+2$

1,995   2,000   2,002

1,995 + 5 + 2 = 2,002

1,995 + 7 = 2,002

So, 2,002 − 1,995 = 7

This is how Ebo could have quickly found the answer in his head.

b) To solve 760 − 250 in your head, first partition the number into hundreds and tens.

Subtract the 100s first.

700 − 200 = 500

Then subtract the 10s.

60 − 50 = 10

So, 760 − 250 = 510.

It can be easier to do questions like this in your head rather than using a written method.

I did it a different way. I subtracted 200 to get 560 and then subtracted 50 to get 510.

Think together

1   Match each thought bubble to the calculation that it solves.

Two of the bubbles match to the same calculation.

| 76 – 40 | 76 – 42 | 72 – 46 |

76 – 40 = 36
36 – 2 = 34

72 – 40 = 32
32 – 2 = 30
30 – 4 = 26

76 – 40 = 36

70 – 40 = 30
6 – 2 = 4
30 + 4 = 34

2   a) Work out 506 – 498 by counting on.

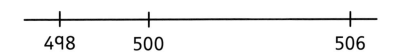

498   500   506

b) Now solve these calculations mentally.

You could try imagining a number line in your head.

| 710 – 697 | 4,302 – 4,299 | 10,005 – 9,987 |

3 Ambika and Andy are using different methods to work out this missing number in their heads.

CHALLENGE

$360 + \boxed{} = 750$

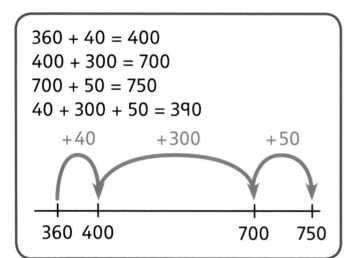

$360 + 40 = 400$
$400 + 300 = 700$
$700 + 50 = 750$
$40 + 300 + 50 = 390$

+40   +300   +50

360 400   700   750

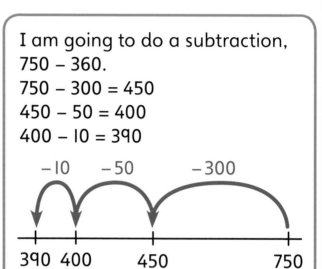

I am going to do a subtraction, $750 - 360$.
$750 - 300 = 450$
$450 - 50 = 400$
$400 - 10 = 390$

−10   −50   −300

390 400   450   750

Ambika

Andy

a) Why do both of these methods work?

b) Which one do you prefer?

I wonder if I can use each of these methods to work out $640 + \boxed{} = 920$.

I think I have seen one of these methods before, in the previous lesson.

107

Using inverse operations

Discover

1 a) What addition calculations can Reena and Lee do to check their answers? Who is correct?

b) What mistake has the other person made?

Share

a) Reena and Lee can do the following addition calculations to check their answers.

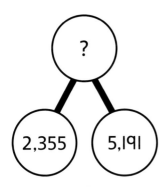

Th	H	T	O
2	3	5	5
+ 5	1	9	1
7	5	4	6
		1	

> I remember that to check a calculation I can use the inverse operation. To check a subtraction, I can use an addition.

Reena is correct as 2,355 + 5,191 is equal to 7,546.

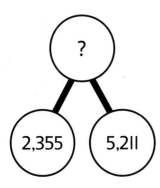

Th	H	T	O
2	3	5	5
+ 5	2	1	1
7	5	6	6

Lee is incorrect as 2,355 + 5,211 = 7,566 and not 7,546.

b) Lee should have exchanged 1 hundred for 10 tens so that he could do the subtraction.

Lee's method

Th	H	T	O
7	5	4	6
− 2	3	5	5
5	2	1	1

Correct method

Th	H	T	O
7	⁴5̷	¹4	6
− 2	3	5	5
5	1	9	1

Think together

1 Reena and Lee are now working out 23,405 + 7,892.

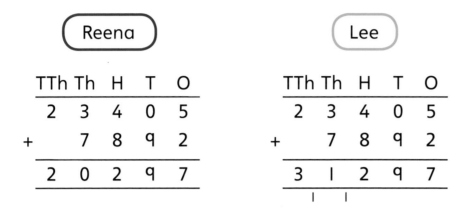

	Reena						Lee			
TTh	Th	H	T	O		TTh	Th	H	T	O
2	3	4	0	5		2	3	4	0	5
+	7	8	9	2		+	7	8	9	2
2	0	2	9	7		3	1	2	9	7

a) Who has the correct answer? How can you check the answer is correct?

b) What mistake has the other person made?

2 Reena and Lee are now working out 46,795 – 3,548.

	Reena						Lee			
TTh	Th	H	T	O		TTh	Th	H	T	O
4	6	7	9	5		4	6	7	9	5
– 3	5	4	8			–	3	5	4	8
1	1	3	1	5		4	3	2	5	3

Use addition to check Reena and Lee's answers.

What mistakes have been made?

I wonder if I could use an estimate instead to check if Reena's answer is correct.

3 **a)** Write the fact family for this part-whole model.

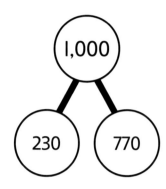

b) What two subtractions would help you to check this calculation?

$$3,270 + 7,730 = 10,000$$

c) Work out the answers to your two subtractions to check that the calculation is correct.

To subtract a number from 10,000 I might subtract 1 from each number first.

A part-whole model will help me work out the fact family.

III

Problem solving – addition and subtraction ❶

Discover

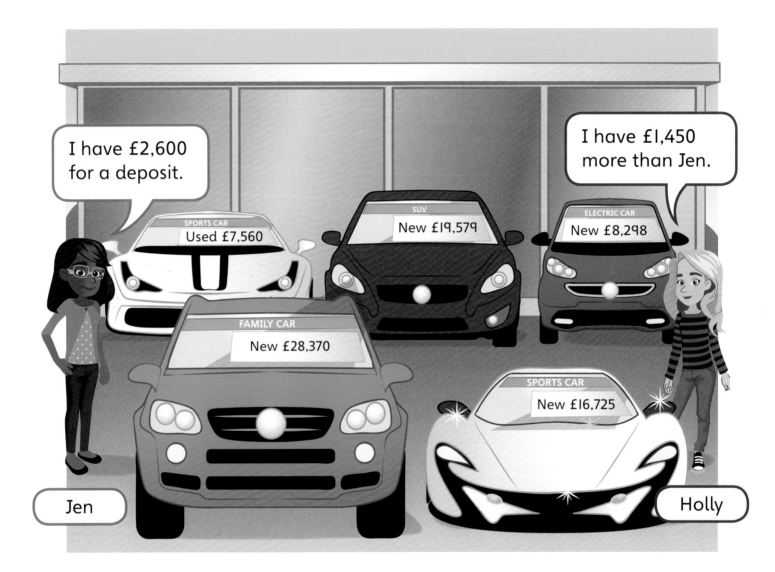

I have £2,600 for a deposit.

I have £1,450 more than Jen.

SPORTS CAR
Used £7,560

SUV
New £19,579

ELECTRIC CAR
New £8,298

FAMILY CAR
New £28,370

SPORTS CAR
New £16,725

Jen

Holly

❶ a) What is the difference in the price between the cost of the new sports car and the used one?

b) How much money do Jen and Holly have altogether?

Share

a) 16,725 − 7,560

I will use bar models to help me. I can see that I need to do subtraction as I am finding a difference.

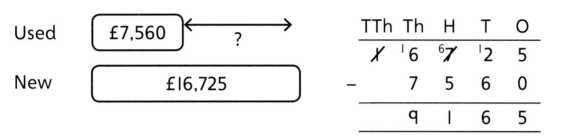

		TTh	Th	H	T	O
		$\cancel{1}$	^{16}	$^6\cancel{7}$	^{12}	5
−			7	5	6	0
			9	1	6	5

The difference in the price between the cost of the new sports car and the used one is £9,165.

b) Jen has £2,600 and Holly has £1,450 more than Jen.

I know that I need to work out how much money Holly has first.

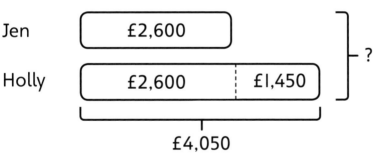

	Th	H	T	O
	2	6	0	0
+	1	4	5	0
	4	0	5	0
		1		

£2,600 + £1,450 = £4,050

	Th	H	T	O
	2	6	0	0
+	4	0	5	0
	6	6	5	0

£2,600 + £4,050 = £6,650

Jen and Holly have £6,650 altogether.

Think together

1 Together, Jen and Holly want to buy the new sports car.

How much more money do they need?

£16,725

	£6,650	?

TTh	Th	H	T	O
1	6	7	2	5
−	6	6	5	0

Jen and Holly need £ [ ] more to buy the new sports car.

2 How much do these three cars cost in total?

FAMILY CAR
New £28,370

SUV
New £19,579

SPORTS CAR
New £16,725

Explain your method.

?

£19,579	£28,370	£16,725

These three cars cost £ [ ] in total.

3 How much more does the family car cost than the combined total cost of the SUV and the electric car?

CHALLENGE

FAMILY CAR
New £28,370

ELECTRIC CAR
New £8,298

SUV
New £19,579

I think I need to do an addition and then a subtraction to work this out.

I will try and represent this as a bar model. I will use one that helps me to show a comparison.

115

Problem solving – addition and subtraction ❷

Discover

I **a)** How much fuel has the plane used so far?

b) Each hour the plane uses 13,580 litres of fuel.

How much fuel will be left after two more hours of flying?

Share

a)

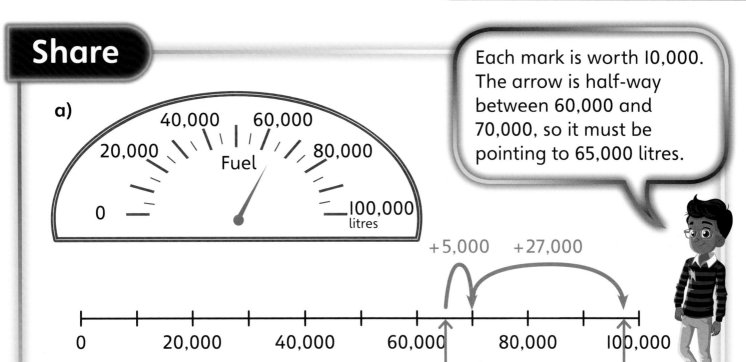

Each mark is worth 10,000. The arrow is half-way between 60,000 and 70,000, so it must be pointing to 65,000 litres.

$5,000 + 27,000 = 32,000$

The plane has used **32,000** litres of fuel so far.

b) 13,580 litres of fuel are used each hour for two hours.

I did a column subtraction to check the answer.

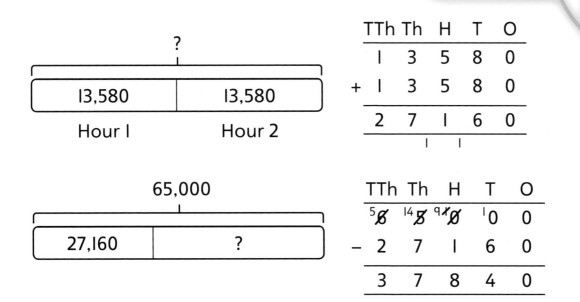

There will be 37,840 litres of fuel left after two more hours of flying.

Think together

1 The table shows the number of passengers passing through an airport on one day.

Did more passengers pass through before 2 pm or after 2 pm?

6 am – 10 am	10 am – 2 pm	2 pm – 6 pm	6 pm – 10 pm
14,569	11,118	5,946	23,277

More passengers passed through the airport _____ 2 pm.

2 A large plane carries 416 passengers.

A small plane carries 280 fewer passengers.

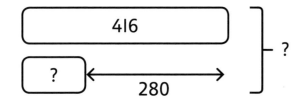

How many passengers can the two planes carry in total?

The two planes can carry ☐ passengers in total.

> I did a column subtraction to check my answer.

3 A pilot uses this information to work out how much fuel a plane needs.

Take off fuel	5,600 litres
Flight fuel	12,500 litres per hour
Landing fuel	5,150 litres
Spare fuel	2,500 litres per hour

How much fuel will the pilot need for a 4-hour flight?

There seems to be a lot of adding here.

I think I can make parts of the calculation easier.

→ Practice book 5A p85

End of unit check

1 What is 16,762 + 3,511?

A 19,273   B 41,872   C 51,872   D 20,273

2 Which number is missing from this calculation?

7,600 + ☐ = 10,000

A 17,600   B 3,400   C 2,400   D 12,400

3 Kate has £1,260.

Mark has £275 more than Kate.

How much money do they have altogether?

A £2,255   B £2,795   C £995   D £1,535

4 What is eighty less than three hundred thousand?

A 200,020   B 299,920   C 299,200   D 209,920

5 What is the difference between X and Y?

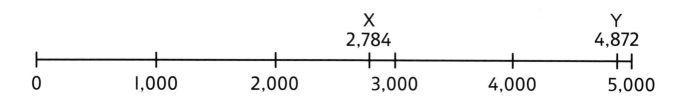

A 216   **B** 1,216   **C** 2,088   **D** 7,656

6 The distance from Earth to the Moon is 384,000 km.

A rocket travels 138,000 km each day.

How many days will it take to reach the Moon?

It will take ☐ days to reach the Moon.

7 There are 4,500 trees in a forest.

1,219 trees are cut down.

2,175 trees are planted.

How many trees are in the forest now?

There are ☐ trees in the forest now.

→ Practice book 5A p88

Unit 4
Graphs and tables

In this unit we will …

⚡ Read information from tables

⚡ Understand and create two-way tables

⚡ Read information from line graphs

⚡ Answer questions relating to the information in graphs and tables

⚡ Draw simple line graphs

You will be able to draw a line graph from data in a table. Can you see how the line graph has been drawn?

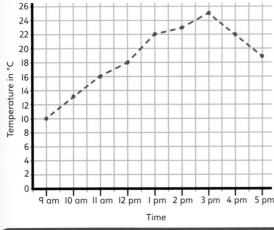

Time	9 am	10 am	11 am	12 pm	1 pm	2 pm	3 pm	4 pm	5 pm
Temp (°C)	10	13	16	18	22	23	25	22	19

We will need some maths words.
How many of these can you remember?

graph   line graph   table

dual line graph   horizontal   vertical

two-way table   scale   axis/axes

data   kilometres (km)   kilograms (kg)

plot/plotted   tallies/tally   digits

You can think of the axes like number lines. What numbers are missing from the number line? What are the arrows pointing to?

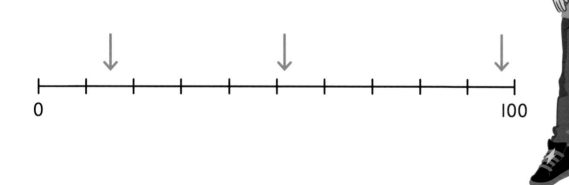

0   100

Interpreting tables

Discover

Last Week's Sales

Day	Number of loaves sold
Monday	127
Tuesday	195
Wednesday	88
Thursday	152
Friday	123

1 **a)** In total, how many loaves were sold on Monday and Thursday?

b) The bakery makes 200 loaves every day.

How many loaves were **not** sold on Friday?

Share

a)

Day	Number of loaves sold
Monday	127
Tuesday	195
Wednesday	88
Thursday	152
Friday	123

?

127	152

I used column addition to work out the total.

```
  H  T  O
  1  2  7
+ 1  5  2
─────────
  2  7  9
```

127 loaves of bread were sold on Monday.

152 loaves of bread were sold on Thursday.

In total, 279 loaves of bread were sold on Monday and Thursday.

b) 200 loaves of bread were made on Friday.

123 loaves of bread were sold on Friday.

Method 1

200

123	?

```
  H  T  O
  ¹2 ⁹9 ¹0
-  1  2  3
─────────
  0  7  7
```

Method 2

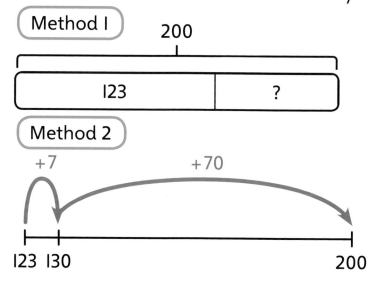

+7   +70

123 130   200

I used a number line to work out what I needed to add on.

77 loaves were **not** sold on Friday.

Think together

1 The table shows the weight of five dogs.

Name	Arnie	Buddy	Charlie	Digga	Ernie
Weight (kg)	23	19	26	23	20

a) How much does Ernie weigh?

Ernie weighs ☐ kg.

b) Which two dogs are the same weight?

Both _____ and _____ are the same weight.

c) How much more does Charlie weigh than Buddy?

Charlie weighs ☐ kg. Buddy weighs ☐ kg.

☐ – ☐ = ☐

Charlie weighs ☐ kg more than Buddy.

d) The vet says a dog is overweight if it weighs more than 24 kg. Are any of the dogs overweight? If so, which ones?

e) Another dog, Rufus, has a weight that is in between Buddy's and Ernie's weight. How much could Rufus weigh?

Rufus could weigh ☐ kg.

2 The table shows how many kilometres (km) Lexi walks each day.

Day	Mon	Tue	Wed	Thur	Fri
Distance (km)	5	6	3·5	7·5	

Lexi wants to walk 30 km in total.

How many more kilometres does she need to walk on Friday?

Lexi needs to walk ☐ more kilometres on Friday.

3·5 is the same as $3\frac{1}{2}$.

3 Children were asked to choose their favourite colour.

CHALLENGE

Favourite colour	Number of children
Pink	12
Blue	10
Red	11
Green	4
Yellow	2
Other	1

I remember from my work earlier that to find $\frac{1}{4}$ I divide by 4.

The results were put into a table.

Holly says that more than $\frac{1}{4}$ of the children preferred blue.

Is Holly correct? Explain how you know.

I will halve and halve again.

127

Two-way tables

Discover

1 **a)** Amal wants to sort out the socks from the hats and the spots from the stripes. Complete the **two-way table** to help him.

	Spots	Stripes
Socks		
Hats		

b) How many more socks than hats are there?

How did you find out your answer?

Share

a)

I used tallies. The first item is a sock that has stripes. I put this in the row that says socks and the column that says stripes.

	Spots	Stripes
Socks	~~IIII~~ III	IIII
Hats	III	~~IIII~~

	Spots	Stripes
Socks	8	4
Hats	3	5

A two-way table shows two or more different sets of information.

b)

	Spots	Stripes	Total
Socks	8	4	12
Hats	3	5	8
Total	11	9	20

There are 12 socks and 8 hats.

12 − 8 = 4

There are 4 more socks than hats.

First, I worked out the total for each of the rows and each of the columns.

129

Think together

1. The two-way table shows information about 50 people who went to the cinema last weekend.

	Saturday	Sunday	Total
Children	5	21	26
Adults	17	7	☐
Total	22	☐	50

a) Fill in the missing totals then answer the following questions.

b) How many children went to the cinema on Saturday?

☐ children went to the cinema on Saturday.

c) In total, how many people went to the cinema on Sunday?

In total, ☐ people went to the cinema on Sunday.

d) On Sunday, how many more children than adults went to the cinema?

☐ more children than adults went to the cinema on Sunday.

e) On which day did the greatest number of people go to the cinema?

The greatest number of people went to the cinema

on _____ .

2 Two classes each have a fruit bowl.

The two-way table shows the fruit in each bowl.

Work with a partner to:

a) Complete the two-way table.

b) Write down five pieces of information the table shows you.

	Apples	Pears	Total
Class 5A	☐	18	30
Class 5B	14	☐	24
Total	26	28	☐

Use words such as total, difference, more and less.

3 The two-way table shows information on the number of ice creams sold.

CHALLENGE

a) Complete the two-way table.

b) What fraction of the ice creams sold were large cones?

		Cone size			
		Small	Medium	Large	Total
Flavour	**Strawberry**	2	12	42	☐
	Chocolate	☐	1	2	11
	Vanilla	☐	49	☐	☐
	Total	☐	☐	50	150

I know the total number of ice creams sold and how many large cones were sold.

→ **Practice book 5A p93**

Interpreting line graphs ①

Discover

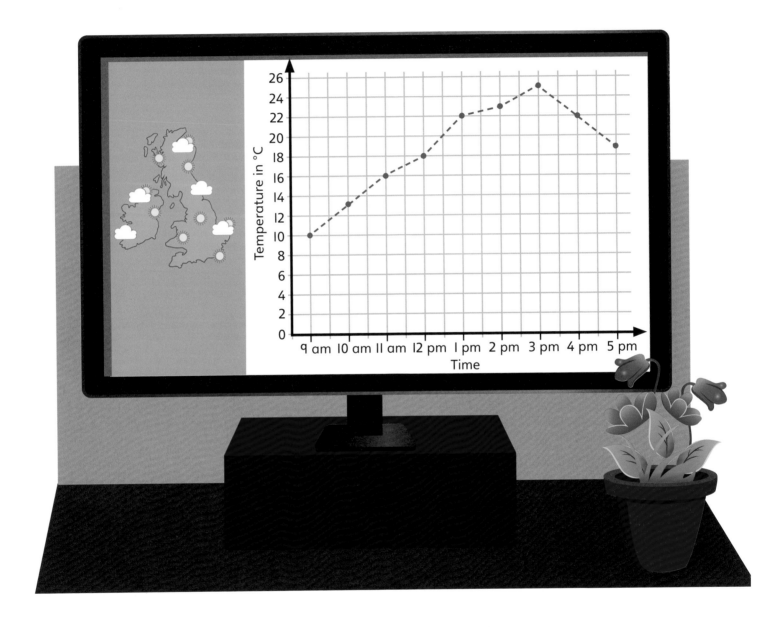

① **a)** What was the temperature at 11 am?

What was the temperature at 2 pm?

b) At which two times was the temperature 22 °C?

Share

a)

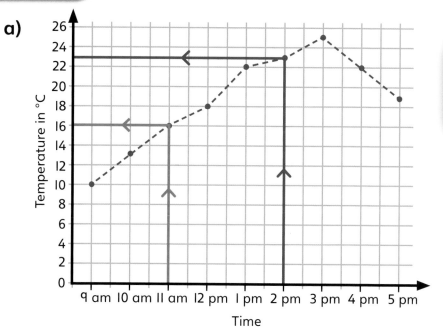

I drew vertical lines up and horizontal lines across to read the correct temperature.

The temperature at 11 am was 16 °C.

The temperature at 2 pm was half-way between 22 °C and 24 °C, so it was 23 °C.

b)

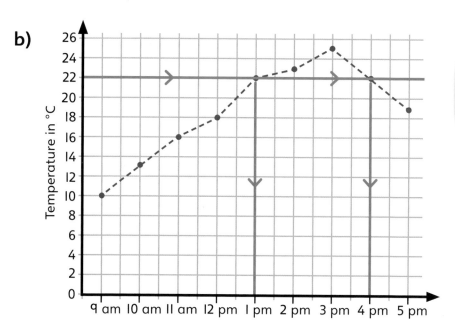

I will start by finding 22 °C on the vertical axis.

The line graph shows that the temperature was 22 °C at 1 pm and at 4 pm.

Think together

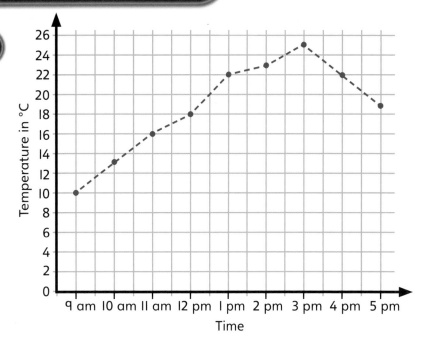

a) What was the highest recorded temperature during the day?

The highest recorded temperature during the day was ☐ °C.

b) Estimate what the temperature was at 11:30 am.

The temperature at 11:30 am was about ☐ °C.

c) Estimate how long the temperature was above 20 °C.

The temperature was above 20 °C for about ☐ hours.

I think I can use the same method that I used to find the times when the temperature was 22 °C.

2 The line graph shows the number of children who were late during a week of school.

   a) How many children were late on Thursday?

   b) How many more children were late on Monday than on Tuesday?

   c) Is Mr Jones's comment correct?

CHALLENGE

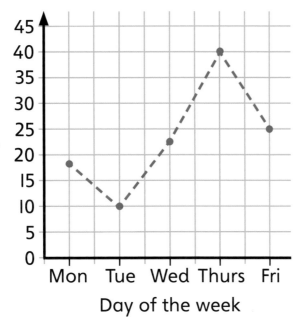

Number of children who were late

Day of the week

The graph shows that 100 different children were late this week.

Mr Jones

I am going to work out the number of children late each day and record it in a table.

I think the total is over 100, but I am not sure that means 100 different children were late in the week.

135

→ Practice book 5A p96

Interpreting line graphs ❷

Discover

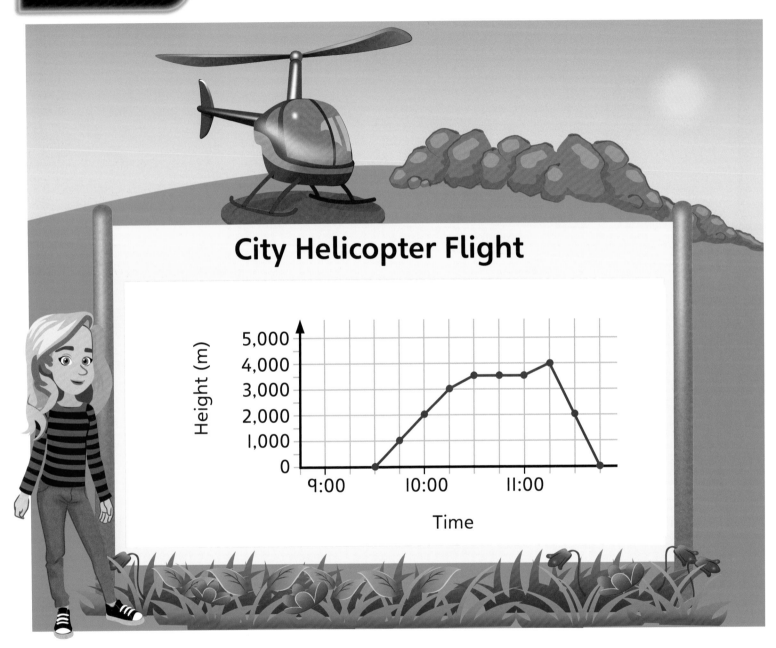

1 a) What is the height of the helicopter at 10:30 am?

How long does the helicopter stay at this height?

b) How long does the helicopter flight last?

Share

a)

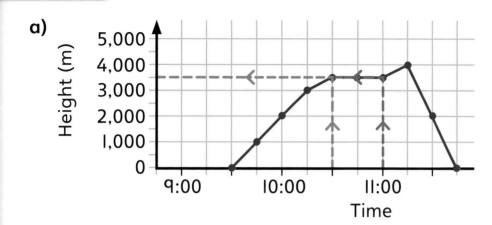

I drew a line up from 10:30 am and across to the height. The height is half-way between 3,000 and 4,000 metres.

I highlighted the graph where it shows the helicopter flying at 3,500 metres. This is a horizontal line.

The height of the helicopter at 10:30 am is 3,500 metres.

The helicopter stays at this height from 10:30 am to 11:00 am.

This is half an hour or 30 minutes.

b) The helicopter flight starts at 9:30 am. The flight finishes at 11:45 am.

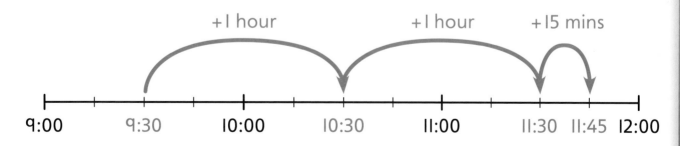

The helicopter flight lasts 2 hours and 15 minutes or $2\frac{1}{4}$ hours.

Think together

A **dual line graph** shows two sets of information on the same graph.

1 This dual line graph shows the average daily temperature in two cities.

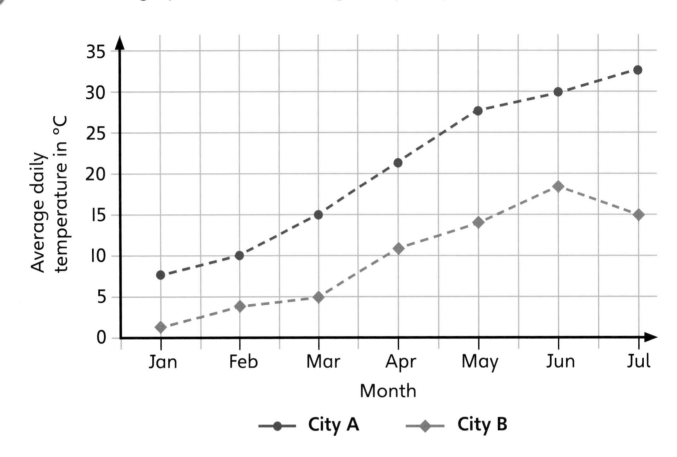

a) What is the temperature in City A in March? ☐ °C

b) What is the temperature in City B in June? ☐ °C

c) In April, how many degrees warmer is it in City A than in City B?

In April, City A is ☐ °C warmer than City B.

d) Which city is warmer?

City ☐ is warmer.

Explain to your partner how the graph shows this.

2 Toshi and Jen are flying a drone.

Here is a graph that shows the journey of the drone.

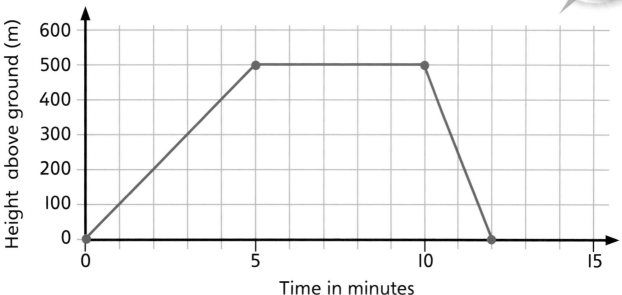

Which of the following statements are true? Explain your reasons.

- The drone starts from the ground.

- For the first 5 minutes, the drone's height increases by 100 metres every minute.

- When it reaches 500 metres the drone flies at this height for 7 minutes.

- The drone returns to the ground after 15 minutes in the air.

I will check the start and finish times and the heights after each minute to find the increase in height and to see how long the drone stays at the same height.

The graph line will tell me how long the drone stayed at the same height and if the height increased at the same rate.

139

Drawing line graphs

Discover

Day	Mon	Tues	Wed	Thurs	Fri	Sat	Sun
Number of cars sold	8	5	7	12	15	19	17

I want a line graph of our car sales from last week.

1 **a)** The sales people have been asked to draw a line graph.

What should they think about before they start?

b) Draw a line graph to show the car sales data.

Share

a)

> I think the days should go on the horizontal axis and sales on the vertical axis.

Amal

> We need to work out a scale for the sales. I think we should go from 0 to 20 in 2s. Otherwise the graph might be too big.

Holly

Before drawing the graph the sales people need to think about:

- what they show on each of the axes
- the scale on each of the axes.

b)

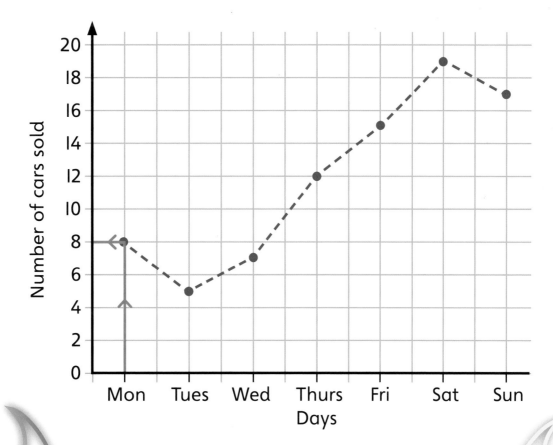

> I drew and labelled the two axes first.

> I plotted each point. For Monday, I plotted my point at 8 because 8 cars were sold on Monday.

Think together

1 Mr Jones sells ice creams.

Day	Ice creams sold
Monday	7
Tuesday	15
Wednesday	22
Thursday	29
Friday	37

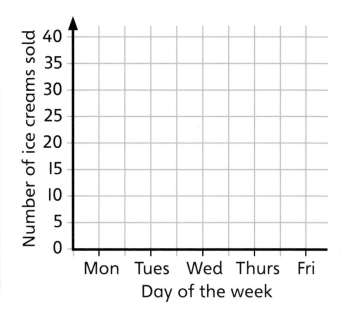

The table shows the number of ice creams he sold last week.

Plot this information on a line graph using squared paper.

2 Mr Jones also measured the temperature each day last week.

The line graph shows the temperature Mr Jones measured each day.

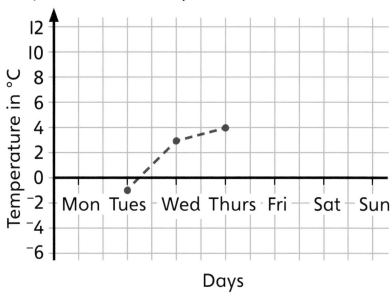

a) The temperature on Monday was ⁻3 °C.

The temperature on Friday was 11 °C.

Complete this graph using squared paper.

b) Use the information on these two line graphs to compare the temperatures with the ice cream sales. What do you notice?

3 Danny collected some information about the population of his village and recorded it in this table.

He then drew this line graph using the information from the table.

Year	2010	2011	2012	2013	2014	2015	2016
Population	750	809	625	500	510	395	450

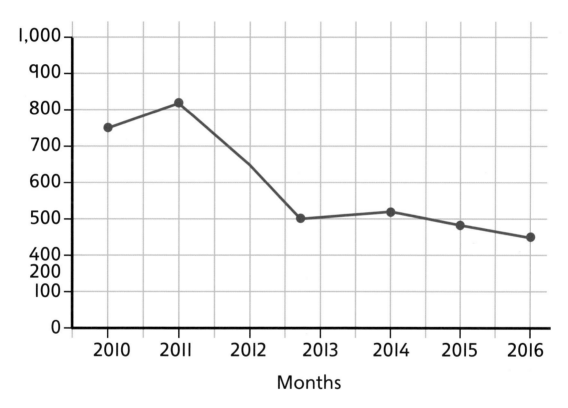

List all of the mistakes Danny has made in plotting and labelling his graph.

I will check whether the graph and the table show the same data.

I wonder if it is more useful to present this information in a graph or a table.

143

End of unit check

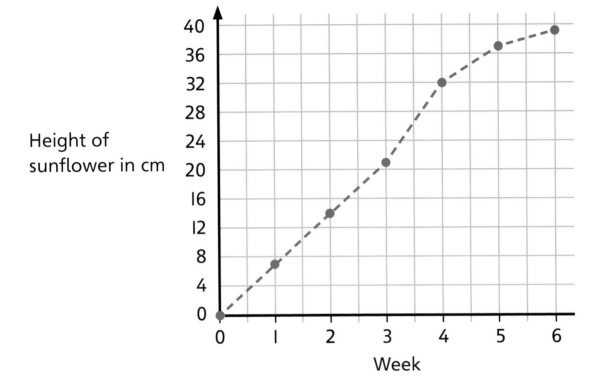

Height of sunflower in cm

Week

1 What is the height of the sunflower after 2 weeks?

A 12 cm   B 13 cm   C 14 cm   D 15 cm

2 How many cm does the flower grow between the start of Week 3 and the start of Week 5?

A 16 cm   B 21 cm   C 39 cm   D 60 cm

100 children were asked to choose their favourite sport.

The table shows the results.

Sport	Number of children
Football	40
Hockey	17
Rounders	12
Other sports	

3 How many children chose other sports?

A 0

C 41

B 31

D I cannot work it out.

4 How many more children chose football than rounders?

A 23

B 28

C 38

D 52

5 The table shows the number of children in a show.

	Singers	Dancers
Boys	12	23
Girls	15	14

A member of the audience says, 'Over a quarter of the children in the show are girl singers.'

Is this true or false? Explain your answer.

→ Practice book 5A p105

Unit 5
Multiplication and division ①

In this unit we will ...

- ⚡ Recognise and find multiples and factors
- ⚡ Recognise and identify prime numbers
- ⚡ Calculate square and cube numbers
- ⚡ Use inverse operations
- ⚡ Multiply and divide by 10, 100 and 1,000
- ⚡ Multiply and divide by multiples of 10, 100 and 1,000

Do you know what these are called? We will use them to help us find factors!

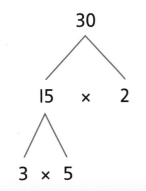

30
15 × 2
3 × 5

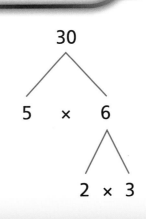

30
5 × 6
2 × 3

We will need some maths words. Look for the words you do not already know. What might they mean?

prime number   composite number

square number   cube number   square (x^2)

cube (x^3)   inverse operation   multiply

divide   multiple   factor   prime factor

We will use multiplication squares too! They will help us spot patterns in the numbers we learn about!

×	1	2	3	4	5	6	7	8	9	10	11	12
1	1	2	3	4	5	6	7	8	9	10	11	12
2	2	4	6	8	10	12	14	16	18	20	22	24
3	3	6	9	12	15	18	21	24	27	30	33	36
4	4	8	12	16	20	24	28	32	36	40	44	48
5	5	10	15	20	25	30	35	40	45	50	55	60
6	6	12	18	24	30	36	42	48	54	60	66	72
7	7	14	21	28	35	42	49	56	63	70	77	84
8	8	16	24	32	40	48	56	64	72	80	88	96
9	9	18	27	36	45	54	63	72	81	90	99	108
10	10	20	30	40	50	60	70	80	90	100	110	120
11	11	22	33	44	55	66	77	88	99	110	121	132
12	12	24	36	48	60	72	84	96	108	120	132	144

Multiples

Discover

1 a) Show all of the multiples of 4 on a 100 square.

b) Do you agree with Luis that 74 is a multiple of 4 because it ends in 4?

Explain your answer to a friend.

Share

I found multiples of 4 by multiplying by 4.

You can also count in 4s.

a)

1	2	3	4	5	6	7	8	9	10
11	12	13	14	15	16	17	18	19	20
21	22	23	24	25	26	27	28	29	30
31	32	33	34	35	36	37	38	39	40
41	42	43	44	45	46	47	48	49	50
51	52	53	54	55	56	57	58	59	60
61	62	63	64	65	66	67	68	69	70
71	72	73	74	75	76	77	78	79	80
81	82	83	84	85	86	87	88	89	90
91	92	93	94	95	96	97	98	99	100

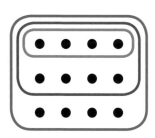

$1 \times 4 = 4$

$2 \times 4 = 8$

$3 \times 4 = 12$

…

20 21 22 23 24 25 26 27 28 29 30 31 32

b) If a number divides by 4 with no remainder, then it is a multiple of 4.

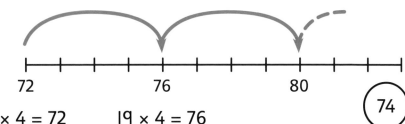

$4 \div 4 = 1$

$8 \div 4 = 2$

$12 \div 4 = 3$

…

Some numbers that end in 4 are multiples of 4, such as 24, 44 and 84.

But it is not always true. For example: 14, 34, 54 are not multiples of 4.

72   76   80

$18 \times 4 = 72$ $19 \times 4 = 76$

$74 \div 4 = 18$ remainder 2

Luis is incorrect as 74 is not a multiple of 4.

74
40 32 2

$40 \div 4 = 10$

$32 \div 4 = 8$

So $74 \div 4 = 18$ r 2

Think together

A multiple of a number is that number multiplied by another number.

1 Using a 100 square, show all of the multiples of 2. What do you notice about the numbers that are not multiples of 2?

Multiples of 2 have _____ in the ones digit.

Numbers that are multiples of 2 are all _____ .

Numbers that are **not** multiples of 2 are all _____ .

I know which numbers leave a remainder when you divide by 2.

1	②	3	④	5	⑥	7	⑧	9	⑩
11	⑫	13	⑭	15	⑯	17	⑱	19	⑳
21	22	23	24	25	26	27	28	29	30
31	32	33	34	35	36	37	38	39	40
41	42	43	44	45	46	47	48	49	50
51	52	53	54	55	56	57	58	59	60
61	62	63	64	65	66	67	68	69	70
71	72	73	74	75	76	77	78	79	80
81	82	83	84	85	86	87	88	89	90
91	92	93	94	95	96	97	98	99	100

2 Using a 100 square, find all of the multiples of 5. Make a list of the multiples of 5.

Multiples of 5 have _____ in the ones digit.

Even multiples of 5 all end in _____ .

Odd multiples of 5 all end in _____ .

1	2	3	4	5	6	7	8	9	10
11	12	13	14	15	16	17	18	19	20
21	22	23	24	25	26	27	28	29	30
31	32	33	34	35	36	37	38	39	40
41	42	43	44	45	46	47	48	49	50
51	52	53	54	55	56	57	58	59	60
61	62	63	64	65	66	67	68	69	70
71	72	73	74	75	76	77	78	79	80
81	82	83	84	85	86	87	88	89	90
91	92	93	94	95	96	97	98	99	100

3 **a)** Find two numbers to go in each section of this table.

CHALLENGE

	Multiple of 6	Not a multiple of 6
Ends in a 6		
Does not end in a 6		

b) 'If a number ends in a 6, then it is a multiple of 6.'

Is this always true, sometimes true or never true?

c) Which numbers could you place in these sorting circles?

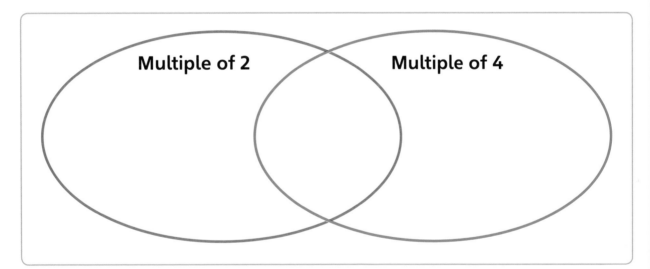

Multiple of 2   Multiple of 4

I will use a 100 square to find the patterns.

I wonder if there will be numbers in every part of the sorting circles.

151

Factors

Discover

> We need to arrange 24 chairs into rows. Each row has the same number of chairs.

 a) Find different ways to arrange the 24 chairs into equal rows.

b) What if there were 25 chairs? Would there be more arrangements?

Share

I used 24 counters to represent the chairs and checked the different arrangements.

a)

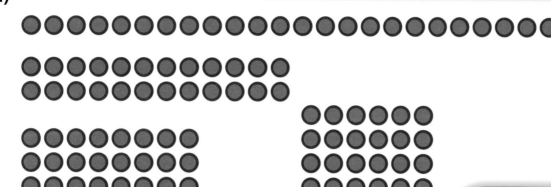

24 chairs can be arranged into equal rows by finding the factors of 24.

Factors are numbers that divide exactly into another number.

$1 \times 24 = 24$ 1 and 24 are factors of 24.
$2 \times 12 = 24$ 2 and 12 are factors of 24.
$3 \times 8 = 24$ 3 and 8 are factors of 24.
$4 \times 6 = 24$ 4 and 6 are factors of 24.

$24 \div 5 = 4$ remainder 4.

There cannot be 5 equal rows, because 5 is not a factor of 24.

When you divide 24 by 5, there is a remainder.

b) By making arrays with counters, we can find the factors of 25.

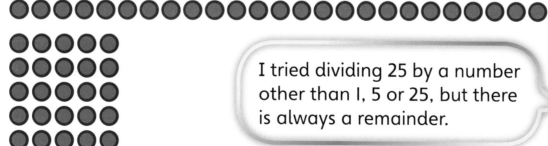

I tried dividing 25 by a number other than 1, 5 or 25, but there is always a remainder.

There are fewer arrangements as there are only 3 factors of 25: 1, 5 and 25.

Think together

1 Using squared paper, find all of the factors of 16 by drawing different arrays. The first array has been done for you.

$16 = 1 \times 16$

$16 = \boxed{} \times \boxed{}$

$16 = \boxed{} \times \boxed{}$

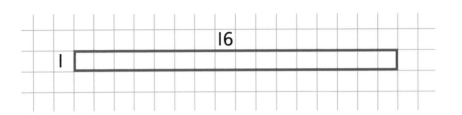

The factors of 16 are _____ .

2 **a)** Is 5 a factor of 16? Use a number line to work this out. Explain the reason.

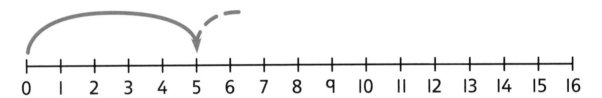

$1 \times 5 = \boxed{}$ $2 \times 5 = \boxed{}$ $3 \times 5 = \boxed{}$ $4 \times 5 = \boxed{}$

5 is / is not a factor of 16 because _____ .

b) Is 4 a factor of 22? Use a number line and division to explain the reason.

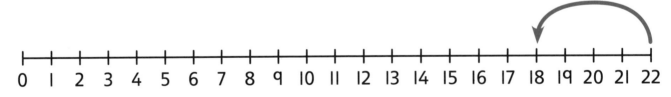

4 is / is not a factor of 22 because _____ .

3 Bella and Aki want to find all of the factors of 30.

CHALLENGE

I will list all of the multiplication facts in order.

Bella

$1 \times 30 = 30$

$2 \times 15 = 30$

$3 \times ...$

I will use division and list the facts in order.

Aki

$30 \div 1 = 30$

$30 \div 2 = 15$

$30 \div ...$

a) Find all of the factors of 30.

b) Find all of the factors of 40. Whose method did you use?

I wonder when they will be able to stop their lists.

155

→ Practice book 5A p111

Prime numbers

Discover

Get into equal groups to practise with no one left out.

1 **a)** What equal groups can the rugby players make?

b) There are 9 tennis players and 7 basketball players.

Which of the sports teams can split into equal groups in more ways?

Share

> I used counters to make arrays, but there was always a remainder.

a)

$13 \div 1 = 13$

$13 \div 2 = 6 \text{ r } 1$ $13 \div 3 = 4 \text{ r } 1$

I and 13 are the only factors of 13.

> I tried to find all of the factors of 13 using division.

The rugby players can only be in 1 group of 13 or 13 groups of 1.

> Numbers with only two factors are called **prime numbers**.
>
> These are special numbers that can only be divided by themselves and 1.

b) 9 has three factors, and can make:

$1 \times 9 = 9$ $3 \times 3 = 9$

The factors of 9 are 1, 3 and 9.

7 is a prime number. It only has two factors and can make:

$1 \times 7 = 7$

The team of tennis players can split into equal groups in more ways than the team of basketball players.

Think together

Numbers which have more than two factors are called **composite numbers**.

1 **a)** What are the factors of 63?

The factors of 63 are _____ .

b) Is 63 a prime number or a composite number?

63 is a _____ number.

2 Think about different numbers of players for a rugby club.

Investigate these numbers and complete the table.
Which are prime numbers?

Number of players	What different arrays can they make?	How many factors?	Is it a prime or composite number?
12			
11			
10			
9	3 × 3, 1 × 9	3	Composite
8			
7	1 × 7	2	Prime
6			
5			
4			
3			
2			

③ Follow the steps below to use a 100 square to find the prime numbers between 0 and 100.

You can cross out 1 because it is not a prime number.

1 has only one factor. Prime numbers have two different factors.

Step 1: start with 1.

Step 2: 2 is a prime number. Circle it, then cross out multiples of 2.

Step 3: 3 is a prime number. Circle it, then cross out multiples of 3.

Step 4: 5 is a prime number. Circle it, then cross out multiples of 5.

Step 5: 7 is a prime number. Circle it, then cross out multiples of 7.

Step 6: circle all numbers that are not crossed out. Are they all prime numbers?

1	2	3	4	5	6	7	8	9	10
11	12	13	14	15	16	17	18	19	20
21	22	23	24	25	26	27	28	29	30
31	32	33	34	35	36	37	38	39	40
41	42	43	44	45	46	47	48	49	50
51	52	53	54	55	56	57	58	59	60
61	62	63	64	65	66	67	68	69	70
71	72	73	74	75	76	77	78	79	80
81	82	83	84	85	86	87	88	89	90
91	92	93	94	95	96	97	98	99	100

I wonder how many even prime numbers there are.

The prime numbers between 0 and 100 are _____ .

There are ☐ prime numbers between 0 and 100.

→ Practice book 5A p114

Using factors

Discover

I want to buy 5 boxes of doughnuts.

Aki

1 **a)** In total, how many doughnuts will Aki buy?

b) There are 4 cakes in a box. There are 5 boxes on each shelf. There are 6 shelves. In total, how many cakes are there?

Think of two ways to solve each problem.

Share

a) $4 \times 6 = 24$

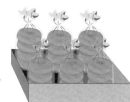

Method 1: There are 24 doughnuts in 1 box.

There are 5 boxes.

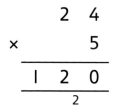

```
    2  4
×      5
─────────
 1  2  0
      2
```

I worked out how many doughnuts are in 1 box, then multiplied that by 5.

Method 2: $5 \times 6 = 30$

There are 30 bags.

In each bag there are 4 doughnuts.

$3 \times 4 = 12$

$30 \times 4 = 120$

I worked out how many bags there are in total.

There are 6 bags in 1 box, and there are 5 boxes.

Both methods calculate $4 \times 6 \times 5 = 120$.

Aki will buy 120 doughnuts in total.

b)

5 × 4 = 20 cakes on each shelf.	There are 5 boxes on each shelf.

There are 6 shelves each with 20 cakes.	5 × 6 = 30 boxes in total. Each box has 4 cakes.
20 × 6 = 120 cakes in total.	30 × 4 = 120 cakes in total.

I solved 30 × 4 by using known facts.

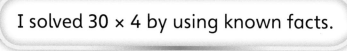

Think together

1 Reena and Luis are working out $2 \times 2 \times 7$.

I did $2 \times 2 = 4$ then calculated 7×4.

Reena

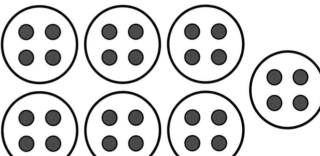

This is my method. $2 \times 7 = 14$.
Then I calculated 14×2.

Luis

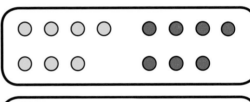

We usually write the factors in increasing order.

a) Use both methods to work out $2 \times 2 \times 7$.

b) Choose a sign to complete this number statement.

$4 \times 7 \bigcirc 2 \times 14$

162

2 **a)** This is a factor tree diagram.

It shows different ways to find the prime factors of 30.

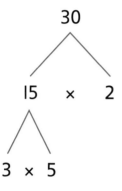   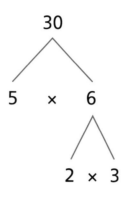

Prime factors are the factors that are also prime numbers.

The branch stops if you reach a prime number.

Calculate 3 × 5 × 2 and 5 × 2 × 3.

Can you multiply the factors in different orders?

I wonder if the order matters when doing multiplication.

b) Factor trees do not always need to find only prime factors.

Complete these factor trees to find different ways to calculate the total.

5 × 5 × 6 = ☐

☐ × ☐ × 25 = ☐

163

Squares

Discover

1 **a)** How many small squares are there on the chessboard altogether?

b) What other size squares can you find on the chessboard?

Share

a) There are 8 rows of 8 squares.

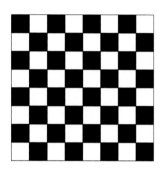

$8 \times 8 = 64$

64 is called a **square number**. It can be found by multiplying a whole number by itself.

There are 64 small squares on the chessboard altogether.

> 8×8 is called '8 squared'.
>
> It can be written as 8^2.
>
> The small ^{2} does not mean multiply by 2. It means 'multiply by itself'.

b) There are squares of different sizes on the chessboard.

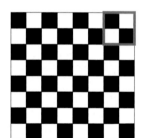 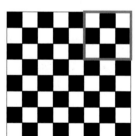 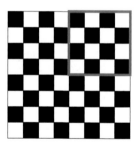

> I know that these are all square numbers!

 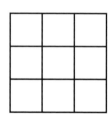 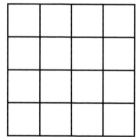

$2 \times 2 = 2^2 = 4$ $3 \times 3 = 3^2 = 9$ $4 \times 4 = 4^2 = 16$

There are also squares of 5×5, 6×6, 7×7 and 8×8.

Think together

1 Complete the number sentences for each array.

a)
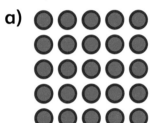

$$\boxed{}^2 = \boxed{} \times \boxed{} = \boxed{}$$

b)
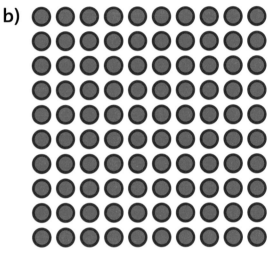

$\boxed{}$ squared is $\boxed{}$.

2 Which square numbers can you find in the multiplication table?

×	1	2	3	4	5	6	7	8	9	10	11	12
1	1	2	3	4	5	6	7	8	9	10	11	12
2	2	(4)	6	8	10	12	14	16	18	20	22	24
3	3	6	(9)	12	15	18	21	24	27	30	33	36
4	4	8	12	(16)	20	24	28	32	36	40	44	48
5	5	10	15	20	25	30	35	40	45	50	55	60
6	6	12	18	24	30	36	42	48	54	60	66	72
7	7	14	21	28	35	42	49	56	63	70	77	84
8	8	16	24	32	40	48	56	64	72	80	88	96
9	9	18	27	36	45	54	63	72	81	90	99	108
10	10	20	30	40	50	60	70	80	90	100	110	120
11	11	22	33	44	55	66	77	88	99	110	121	132
12	12	24	36	48	60	72	84	96	108	120	132	144

The square numbers 4, 9 and 16 are shown in the table. What is the pattern made by the square numbers?

Is 1 a square number? How about 2? Discuss your answers with a partner.

3 **a)** Jamilla thinks 12 is a square number.

Look! I made a square using exactly 12 tiles. It must be a square number.

Jamilla

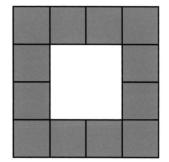

$12 \div 1 = 12$

$12 \div 2 = 6$

$12 \div 3 = 4$

$1 \times 12 = 12$

$2 \times 6 = 12$

$3 \times 4 = 12$

I found all the factors of 12 to check. I do not think it can be a square number.

Isla

Is Jamilla correct?

b) Do you agree or disagree with Astrid? Explain your answer using objects or diagrams.

I do not think 16 is a square number. It makes rectangles, not squares!

167

Cubes

Discover

Do you know a multiplication to work out how many small cubes there are?

PUZZLE CLUB

Zac

Isla

Mrs Dean

Each edge has 2 cubes, which means there are 2 × 2 × 2 cubes in total.

2 × 2 × 2 = 6

1 a) How many small cubes make up the puzzle cube?

b) Explain Isla's mistake.

Share

a)

"I imagined it being split into layers to find the total number of small cubes."

"I split it into towers."

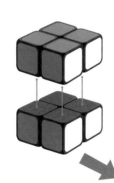

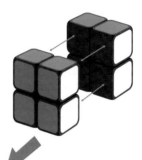

Each layer has 2 × 2 = 4 cubes.

There are 2 layers of 4 cubes.

2 × 2 × 2 = 8

8 small cubes make up the puzzle cube.

"8 is a **cube number**. We can say 2 cubed is equal to 8 or $2^3 = 8$."

b) Isla has made a common mistake.

Isla saw 2 multiplied 3 times, so did 2 × 3 = 6.

"She should have done 2 × 2 = 4 then 4 × 2 = 8."

Think together

1 Amelia has 40 small cubes, and wants to make a bigger cube with these small cubes. What is the largest cube she can make?

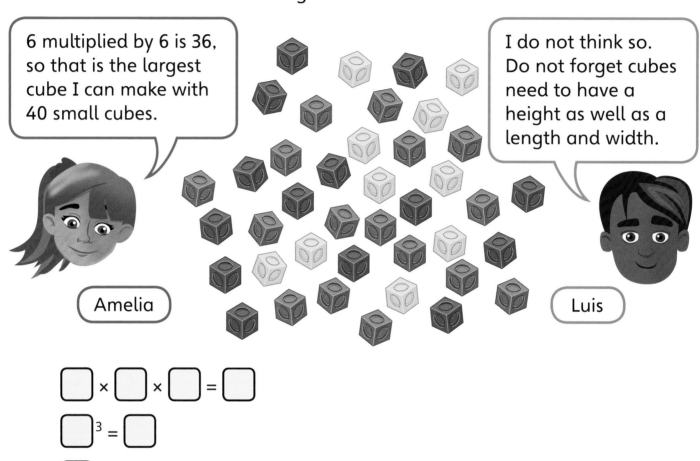

Amelia: 6 multiplied by 6 is 36, so that is the largest cube I can make with 40 small cubes.

Luis: I do not think so. Do not forget cubes need to have a height as well as a length and width.

$\square \times \square \times \square = \square$

$\square^3 = \square$

$\square$ is a cube number.

2 **a)** Complete these calculations.

$1^3 = \square \times \square \times \square = \square$

$10^3 = \square \times \square \times \square = \square$

b) Zac says, 'I worked out $2 \times 2 \times 2$, so 2 is a cube number.'

Explain his mistake.

3 **a)** Now calculate 5^3.

$5^3 = \boxed{}$

There are 25 in each layer.

I need to work out how many layers of 25 are in the full cube.

I know 4 × 25.

That could be useful.

b) Find different ways to calculate 6^3.

6 × 6 in each layer, 6 layers in total, $6^3 = 6 \times 6 \times 6$.

$6 \times 6 \times 6 = 6 \times 2 \times 3 \times 6, \ldots$

6

2   ×   3

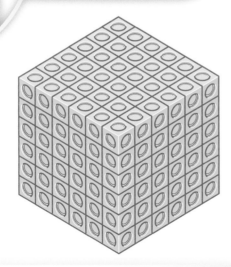

→ **Practice book 5A p123**

Inverse operations

Discover

1. **a)** In total, Emma and Miss Hall need to use 60 stars.

   How many flags will they make?

   b) Miss Hall says they need to use 43 buttons in total.

   Is Miss Hall correct?

Share

a) There are 4 stars on each flag.

I will solve

☐ × 4 = 60.

I will calculate the multiples of 4 until I reach 60.

13 × 4 = 52

14 × 4 = 56

15 × 4 = 60

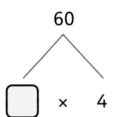

60

☐ × 4

They will make 15 flags.

An **inverse operation** is one that reverses the effect of another operation.

Multiplication and division are inverse operations.

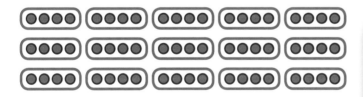

60 ÷ 4 = 15

They will make 15 flags.

I will use the inverse operation.

I will find out how many times 4 goes into 60.

b) Miss Hall is not correct: there cannot be 43 buttons, because 43 is not a multiple of 3.

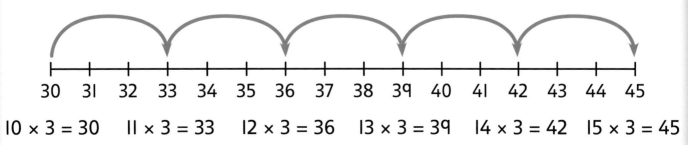

10 × 3 = 30   11 × 3 = 33   12 × 3 = 36   13 × 3 = 39   14 × 3 = 42   15 × 3 = 45

Think together

1 Write multiplication and division facts related to the squares and circles on these flags.

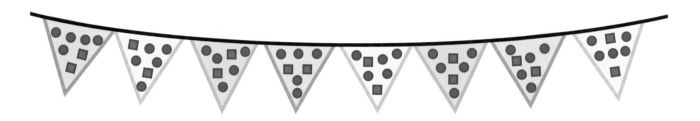

a) Squares

☐ × ☐ = ☐

☐ ÷ ☐ = ☐

☐ ÷ ☐ = ☐

b) Circles

☐ × ☐ = ☐

☐ ÷ ☐ = ☐

☐ ÷ ☐ = ☐

2 Amelia is sewing more bunting. Each flag has 2 stars and some buttons.

a) So far she has used 36 stars.

How many flags has she made?

She has made ☐ flags.

b) She shares her buttons equally, and there are 6 for each flag.

How many buttons did she have?

She had ☐ buttons.

3 **a)** Find the missing values by using inverse operations.

$12 \div 3 = \boxed{}$

$12 \div \boxed{} = 3$

$\boxed{} \times 3 = 12$

$\boxed{} \div 3 = 12$

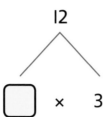

12

$\boxed{}$ × 3

CHALLENGE

I wonder if these are all linked to this factor tree, or if one is different.

b) Think about how you would solve the following calculations.

$22 \div \boxed{} = 2$ $22 \div 2 = \boxed{}$ $\boxed{} \div 2 = 22$ $\boxed{} \div 22 = 2$

What are the different strategies required?

c) What number is Lexi thinking of?

I am thinking of a number. I divide it by 5 and the answer is 3 remainder 3.

Lexi

I wonder if it would help to draw a factor tree, then think about the remainders.

175

Multiplying whole numbers by 10, 100 and 1,000

Discover

Each car needs 4 wheels, 10 batteries, 2 lamps and 12 screws.

I **a)** How many wheels are needed for 10 cars?

How many wheels are needed for 100 cars?

b) How many lamps are needed for 10 cars and then 100 cars?

Share

a) There are 4 wheels for each car, so for 10 cars there are 10 × 4 wheels.

I counted 10 lots of 4.

I grouped in tens, and counted 4 lots of tens.

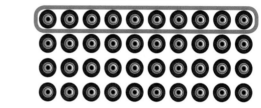

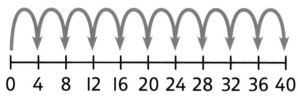

0 4 8 12 16 20 24 28 32 36 40

0   10   20   30   40

It is very useful to know that 10 × 4 = 4 × 10 and 100 × 4 = 4 × 100. You can now multiply by 10 or 100 without counting.

I car	4 × 1 = 4 ones = 4	
10 cars	4 × 10 = 4 tens = 40	
100 cars	4 × 100 = 4 hundreds = 400	

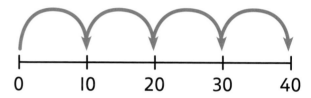

b)

Lamps for I car	Lamps for 10 cars	Lamps for 100 cars
1 × 2 = 2 × 1 = 2	10 × 2 = 2 × 10 = 20	100 × 2 = 2 × 100 = 200

177

Think together

 a) How many batteries are needed for 10 cars? How many for 100 cars? How many for 1,000 cars?

$10 \times 10 = \boxed{}$

$10 \times 100 = \boxed{}$

$10 \times 1,000 = \boxed{}$

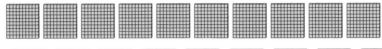
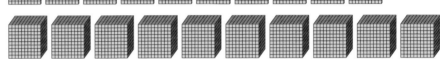

b) How many screws are needed for 10 cars?

$12 \times 10 = \boxed{}$

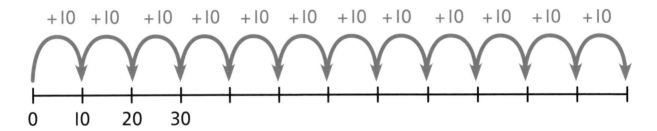

How many screws are needed for 100 cars?

$12 \times 100 = \boxed{}$

How many screws are needed for 1,000 cars?

$12 \times 1,000 = \boxed{}$

2 Aki worked on the following two problems. Do you agree with him?

Explain your reasoning.

$23 \times 100 = 2,300$

$20 \times 100 = 200$

3 **a)** Bella is using a place value grid to work out 10 × 3.

She lays out the following counters

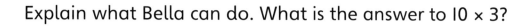

H	T	O
		(30 counters)

Explain what Bella can do. What is the answer to 10 × 3?

b) Multiply each of these numbers by 10.

Explain what happens to the digits.

H	T	O
		3

H	T	O
	1	7

c) Work out 3 × 10 × 10 and 17 × 10 × 10.

I notice that I can exchange the counters.

I think the digit moves columns every time I multiply by 10. I wonder if the counters will help me understand why.

179

→ **Practice book 5A p129**

Dividing whole numbers by 10, 100 and 1,000

Discover

Best shopping rewards ever!

1st prize: 10 winners share total prize of £380

2nd prize: 100 winners share total prize of £1,200

3rd prize: 1,000 winners share total prize of £4,000

Come in for the chance to win!

1 **a)** How much will each 1st prize winner receive?

b) How much will each 2nd prize winner receive?

Share

a) £380 is shared between 10 people.

380

| ? | ? | ? | ? | ? | ? | ? | ? | ? | ? |

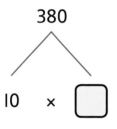
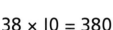

380

10 × ☐

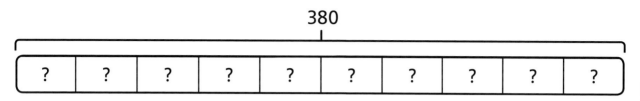

I need to work out 10 × ☐ = 380.

38 × 10 = 380

10 × 38 = 380

I know that 380 is 38 tens.
So, 38 × 10 = 10 × 38 = 380.

380 ÷ 10 = 38

Each 1st prize winner will receive £38.

b) £1,200 is shared between 100 people.

1,200 is 12 hundreds.

Therefore, 1,200 ÷ 100 = 12.

Remember, the inverse operation of multiplication is division.

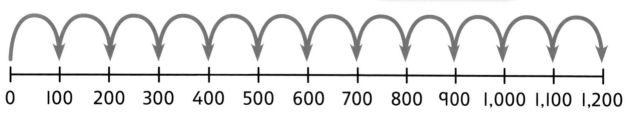

0   100   200   300   400   500   600   700   800   900   1,000   1,100   1,200

Each 2nd prize winner will receive £12.

Think together

1 The total prize money for 3rd prize is £4,000. It is shared between 1,000 people. How much do they each receive?

4,000

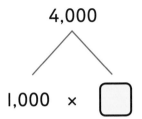

1,000 × ☐

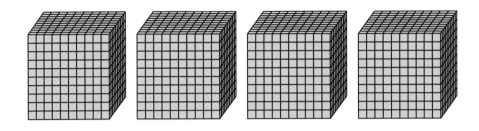

4,000 is ☐ thousands.

☐ × 1,000 = 4,000

4,000 ÷ 1,000 = ☐

Each 3rd prize winner receives £☐ .

2 Solve each of these sets of calculations.

What do you notice?

a) 30 ÷ 10 = ☐

300 ÷ 100 = ☐

3,000 ÷ 1,000 = ☐

c) 300 ÷ 10 = ☐

3,000 ÷ 100 = ☐

30,000 ÷ 1,000 = ☐

b) 310 ÷ 10 = ☐

3,100 ÷ 100 = ☐

31,000 ÷ 1,000 = ☐

3 **a)** Look at the numbers on the place value grids.

Th	H	T	O
4	0	0	0

Th	H	T	O
3	2	0	0

Explain how the numbers change when you divide by 10 or 100.

I will use place value equipment to show the exchange.

b) Max says 'When you divide by 1,000 it is the same as dividing by 10, then by 10 again and then by 10 again.' Do you agree? Explain your answer.

TTh	Th	H	T	O
1	2	0	0	0

→ **Practice book 5A p132**

Multiplying and dividing by multiples of 10, 100 and 1,000

Discover

1 a) How many words does Emma plan to learn in April?

b) What do you think Ebo's method could be?

Share

a) There are 30 days in April. Emma plans to learn 5 × 30 words.

5 × 3 is 15.

5 × 3 tens is 15 tens.

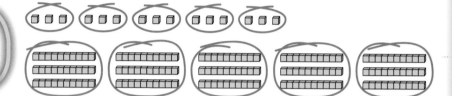

I was going to count 5 jumps of 30, but your way is more efficient.

I can just use my known facts.

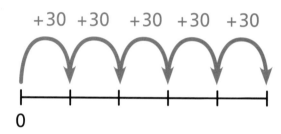

0

5 × 3 = 15

5 × 30 = 150

Emma plans to learn 150 new words in April.

b) Ebo knows that 10 × 30 = 300.

So, he knows 5 × 30 must be half of 300, which is 150.

You can multiply by 5 in two steps: multiplying by 10 and then halving.

10 × 30

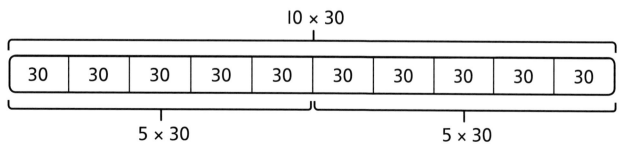

5 × 30   5 × 30

Think together

1 Isla plans to learn 180 French words in April. How many words does she need to learn each day?

$180 \div 30 = \boxed{}$

180 is 18 tens.

30 is 3 tens.

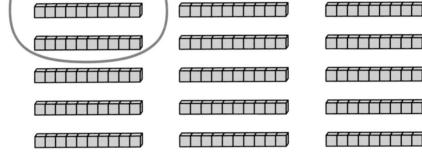

$\boxed{} \times 3 = 18$

$\boxed{} \times 3 \text{ tens} = 18 \text{ tens}$

There are $\boxed{}$ groups of 3 tens in 18 tens.

$180 \div 30 = \boxed{}$, so Isla needs to learn $\boxed{}$ new words each day.

2 Using known number facts from the multiplication table, solve 4×300 and $2,400 \div 600$.

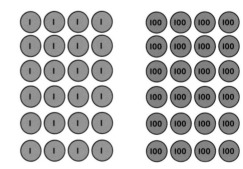

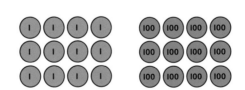

a) $4 \times 3 = \boxed{}$ $4 \times 300 = \boxed{}$

b) $24 \div 6 = \boxed{}$ $2,400 \div 600 = \boxed{}$

186

3 **a)** Two athletes are training for a race.

Athlete A runs 800 m per day for 12 days.

Athlete B runs 600 m per day. How many days will she have to train for before she has run as far as Athlete A?

| 800 | 800 | 800 | 800 | 800 | 800 | 800 | 800 | 800 | 800 | 800 | 800 |

| 600 | |

$800 \times 12 = 600 \times \boxed{}$

Athlete B will have to train for $\boxed{}$ days before she has run as far as Athlete A.

I am not sure about this.
800×12 does not equal 600.
Maybe I need to read it again.

b) Work out the following calculations.

$9 \times 3{,}000 = 90 \times \boxed{}$

$4{,}000 \times \boxed{} = 8 \times 2{,}000$

$35{,}000 \div 7{,}000 = \boxed{} \div 7$

$2{,}400 \div 120 = \boxed{} \div 60$

187

End of unit check

1 Which is both a multiple of 3 and a factor of 60?

A 180   **B** 15   **C** 20   **D** 4

2 Which statement correctly describes the diagram?

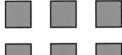

A This shows a prime number because there are an odd number of rows.

B This shows a cube number because it is 3^3.

C This shows that 3 is a square number because there are 3 rows of 3.

D This shows that 9 is a square number, because $3 \times 3 = 9$.

3 Which is **not** equivalent to $5 \times 8 \times 7$?

A 40×7 **B** 40×56 **C** 35×8 **D** 10×28

4 Which of these is not a prime number?

A 2   **B** 17   **C** 31   **D** 39

5 Find the calculation with the answer equivalent to $30 \times 10 \times 10$.

A 50×600 **B** $6,000 \div 20$ **C** 5×60 **D** 150×20

6 Find three prime numbers that complete the following calculation.

$$\boxed{} \times \boxed{} \times \boxed{} = 130$$

7 Here are three digit cards.

$$\boxed{4} \quad \boxed{5} \quad \boxed{7}$$

Debbie makes a 2-digit number and a 1-digit number using the cards.

She multiplies the two numbers together.

The answer is a multiple of 10.

What two numbers did Debbie make?

→ **Practice book 5A p138**

Unit 6
Measure – area and perimeter

In this unit we will ...

⚡ Measure shapes to find their perimeter

⚡ Calculate the perimeter of squares, rectangles and other rectilinear shapes

⚡ Use a formula to find the area of squares and rectangles

⚡ Estimate the area of different shapes

How many rows? How many in each row? How many altogether?

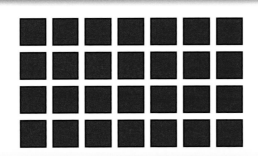

Here are some maths words we will be using. Which words are new?

perimeter   distance   area   space

length   width

centimetres   square centimetres (cm^2)

metres   square metres (m^2)   scale

compare   estimate   formula

2D shape   brackets

Which shape has the largest area? How do you know?

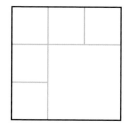 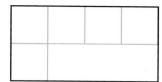 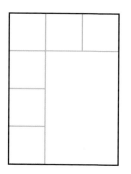

Measuring perimeter

Discover

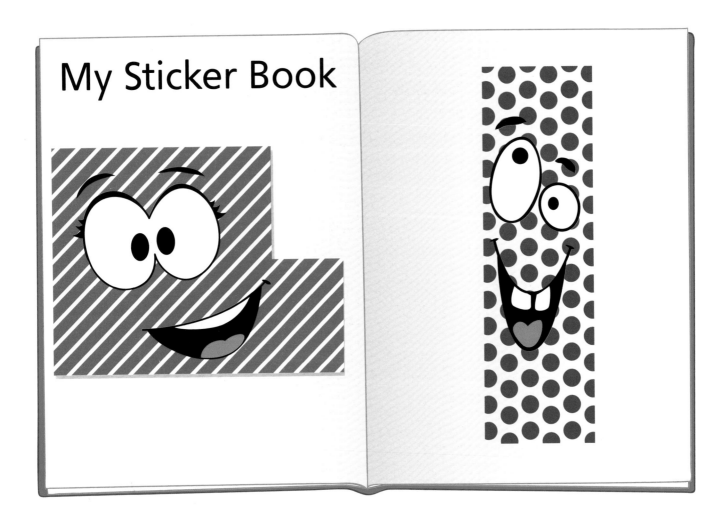

1 **a)** What is the perimeter of the red stripy sticker?

b) Work out the perimeter of the blue dotty sticker without measuring all of the sides.

Share

a)

The perimeter of a 2D shape is the distance all around it.

There are no measurements labelled on the sticker, so I will use a ruler to measure all the sides.

6 cm + 3 cm + 2 cm + 3 cm + 8 cm + 6 cm = 28 cm

The perimeter of the red stripy sticker is 28 cm.

b)

Rectangles have two pairs of equal sides, so I only need to measure two of the sides. I will add these, then double that number.

10 cm + 3 cm = 13 cm

13 × 2 = 26 cm

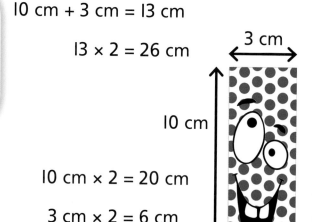

3 cm

10 cm

I doubled the length, doubled the width and added them.

10 cm × 2 = 20 cm

3 cm × 2 = 6 cm

20 + 6 = 26 cm

The perimeter of the blue dotty sticker is 26 cm.

Think together

① What is the perimeter of this sticker?

⬜ cm + ⬜ cm + ⬜ cm +

⬜ cm + ⬜ cm + ⬜ cm +

⬜ cm + ⬜ cm = ⬜ cm

The perimeter is ⬜ cm.

⬜ cm

⬜ cm

⬜ cm

⬜ cm

⬜ cm

⬜ cm

⬜ cm

⬜ cm

⬜ cm

② This sticker was a rectangle. What was its perimeter?

The perimeter of the sticker was ⬜ cm.

Explain how you know.

194

3 You have been asked to find the perimeter of this shape by only measuring two sides.

Point to the two sides you would choose to measure.

Explain how you can use them to find the answer.

I can see some sides that combine together.

The perimeter of the shape is ⬜ cm.

→ Practice book 5A p140

Calculating perimeter ❶

Discover

❶ **a)** What is the perimeter of the football pitch?

b) What is the length of the playground?

Share

a) Jamie and Ebo gave the length and the width of the football pitch.

I am going to sketch a picture to help find the answer.

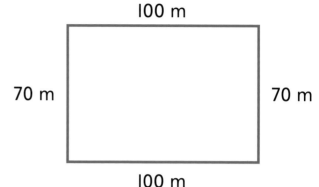

100 m

70 m   70 m

100 m

100 + 70 + 100 + 70 = 340 m

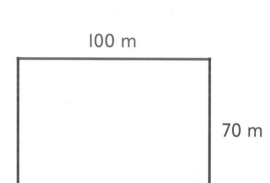

100 m

70 m

I added the length and width and then doubled the result.

100 + 70 = 170

170 × 2 = 340 m

Brackets show which bit of the calculation to do first.

In this example, double the length and double the width before adding them together.

(70 × 2) + (100 × 2)

= 140 + 200

= 340 m

The perimeter of the football pitch is 340 metres.

b) The square playground has four sides all the same length.

perimeter = 200 m			
? m	? m	? m	? m

200 ÷ 4 = 50

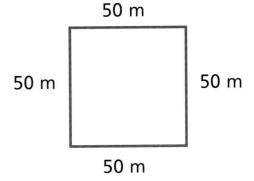
50 m
50 m   50 m
50 m

The length of the playground is 50 metres because 50 m × 4 = 200 m.

Think together

1 A rugby pitch has a width of 70 metres and a length of 120 metres.

What is its perimeter?

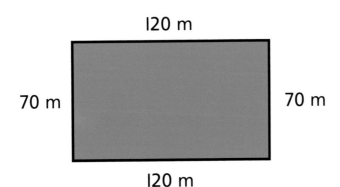
120 m
70 m   70 m
120 m

I could use addition, but I can think of a quicker method using multiplication instead.

(length × 2) + (width × 2)

= (☐ × 2) + (☐ × 2)

= ☐ + ☐

= ☐

The perimeter of the rugby pitch is ☐ metres.

2 **a)** A square car park has a length of 40 metres.

What is its perimeter?

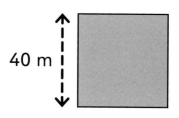

$\boxed{} \times \boxed{} = \boxed{}$

40 m

The perimeter of the car park is $\boxed{}$ metres.

b) A square lawn has a perimeter of 80 metres.

What is its length?

$\boxed{} \div \boxed{} = \boxed{}$

80 m

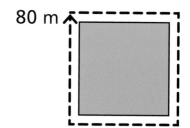

The length of the lawn is $\boxed{}$ metres.

3 The length of a square is 25 cm.

Two squares are put together to make a rectangle.

CHALLENGE

I can't work out the perimeter of the rectangle because I don't know its length.

Amelia

The perimeter of the rectangle is double the perimeter of the square.

Danny

The perimeter of the rectangle is six times the length of the square.

Lee

Who is right? Explain your answer.

I am going to draw a quick sketch to help me work out what the rectangle looks like.

I am not sure if I need to count all the sides. I will check if any sides are inside the rectangle.

199

→ **Practice book 5A p143**

Calculating perimeter ❷

Discover

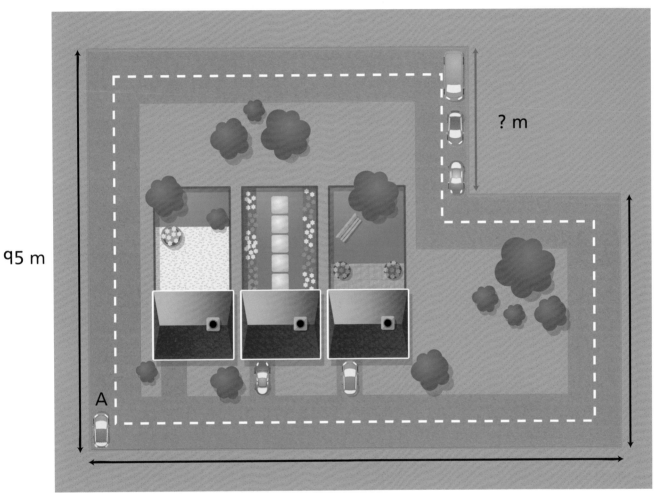

95 m

? m

60 m

130 m

A

1 **a)** How long is the queue of three vehicles?

b) Car A drives all the way around the road once.

How far does it travel?

Share

a)

> I am going to use some of the side lengths I already know to help find the missing length.

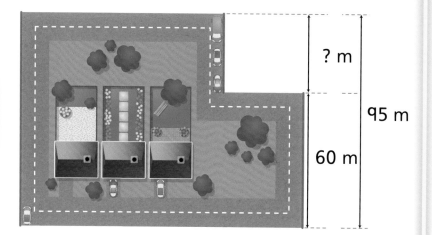

95 m – 60 m = 35 m

The length of the queue of three vehicles is 35 metres.

b) Work out the missing lengths then add to find the distance travelled.

130 + 35 + 60 + 130 + 95 = 450

The car travels
450 metres.

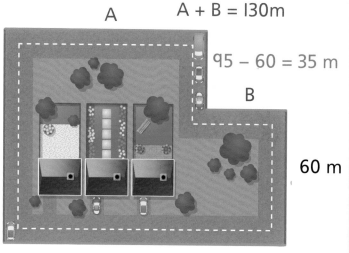

A + B = 130m

95 – 60 = 35 m

95 m

130 m

The sides can combine to make double the length and double the width.

(130 × 2) + (95 × 2) = 260 + 190

= 450

Car A travels 450 metres.

> I found the answer by using doubling!

Think together

1 This is a race track.

a) Complete these number sentences with the correct letters.

$\boxed{} + \boxed{} = 250$ m

$\boxed{} + \boxed{} = 300$ m

b) Find the perimeter of the track.

$(\boxed{} \times 2) + (\boxed{} \times 2)$

$= \boxed{} + \boxed{}$

$= \boxed{}$ m

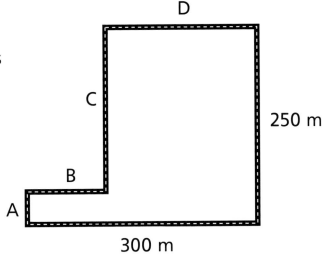

D

C

B

A

250 m

300 m

2 This diagram shows the shape of a playground.

What is the perimeter of the playground?

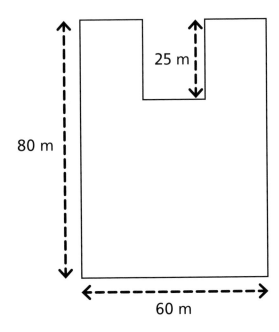

25 m

80 m

60 m

Even though only some of these sides are labelled, I think I can see what the others are equal to.

The perimeter of the playground is $\boxed{}$ m.

3 Lexi has two cardboard rectangles the same size.

42 cm

15 cm

She puts the rectangles together to make a new shape.

What is its perimeter?

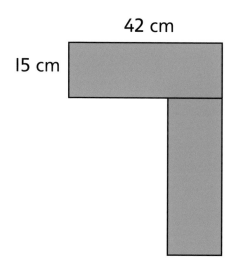

42 cm

15 cm

I know all the side lengths except one.

I have spotted a way to work it out using what I know already.

203

Calculating area ❶

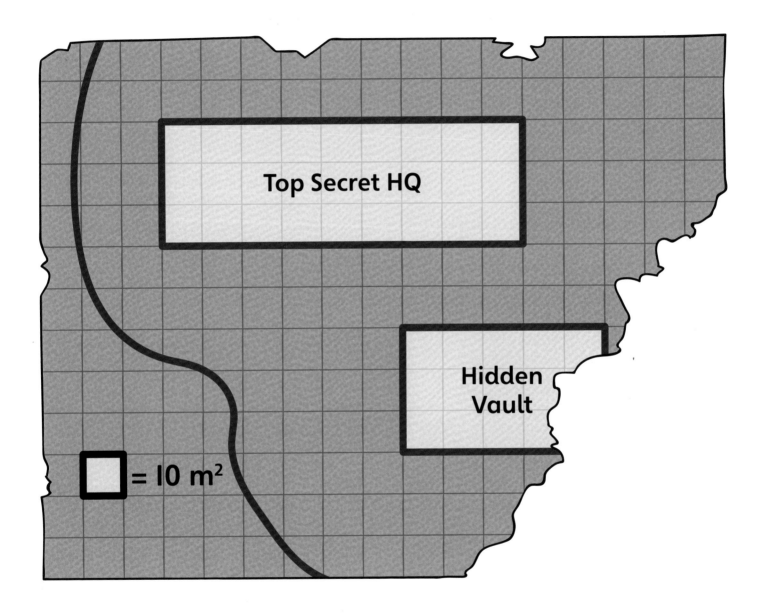

❶ **a)** What is the actual area of the Top Secret HQ?

b) The Hidden Vault is rectangular. What is its actual area?

Share

a) The map is drawn to **scale**.

I square on the map has an area of 10 square metres in real life.

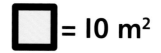 $= 10 \text{ m}^2$

A **square metre** is the area of a I m × I m square. Square metres are written as **m²**.

You can count that there are 27 squares in the rectangle.

I will multiply to find the total area.

$27 \times 10 = 270$

The actual area of the Top Secret HQ is 270 m².

b) The length of the vault is 5 squares

The width of the vault is 3 squares.

There are I5 squares in total.

I know the Hidden Vault is rectangular, so I can predict what the complete shape looks like!

$15 \times 10 = 150$

The actual area of the Hidden Vault is I50 m².

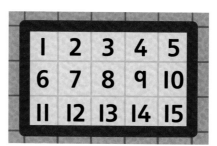

Think together

1 Find the actual area of the Underground Base.

The area of the rectangle on the map is made up of ☐ squares.

Each square is worth ☐ square metres.

You can find the actual area by calculating ☐ × ☐.

The actual area of the Underground Base is ☐ m².

Underground Base

☐ = 100 m²

2 Find the actual areas of these rectangles by counting the squares, then using the scale to help.

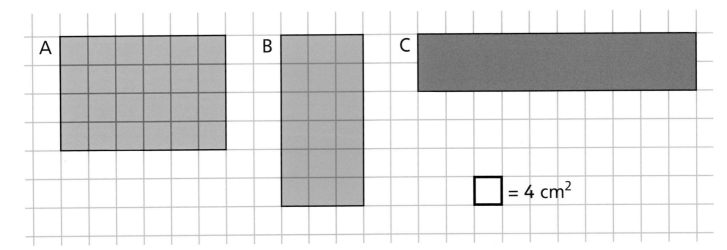

A

B

C

☐ = 4 cm²

a) A = 24 squares × 4 cm² = ☐ cm²

b) B = ☐ squares × 4 cm² = ☐ cm²

c) C = ☐ squares × ☐ cm² = ☐ cm²

> **Square centimetres are written as cm².**

3 These rectangles are drawn to different scales.

Which shape has the smallest actual area?

CHALLENGE

A

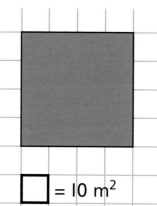

☐ = 10 m²

B

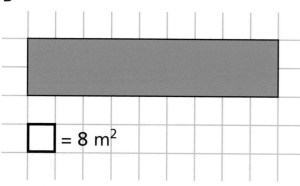

☐ = 8 m²

C

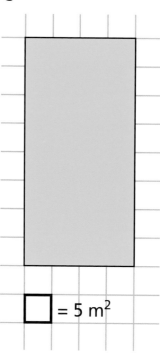

☐ = 5 m²

Explain how you found the correct answer.

I think that the shape with the smallest actual area is the one covering the least squares.

It is not as easy as that! I think that you need to use each scale to calculate the area of each shape before you decide.

207

Calculating area ❷

Discover

1   a) What will the area of Amal's flower bed be?

b) A third gardener digs a rectangular flower bed with an area of 8 m².

   What could its length and width be?

Share

a)

I will find the area by counting each of the squares separately.

The metre squares make a 5 × 4 array. I can use this fact to find the area more quickly!

1   2   3   4

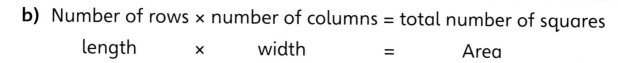

5 m

4 m

You can write a formula for the area of a rectangle.

There are 5 rows of squares.

Each row contains 4 squares.

5 × 4 = 20

There are 20 metre squares altogether.

The area of Amal's flower bed will be 20 m².

Formula for area of a rectangle:
A = l × w

b) Number of rows × number of columns = total number of squares

length   ×   width   =   Area

I think the length and the width must be two numbers that multiply together to make 8.

1 m

8 m

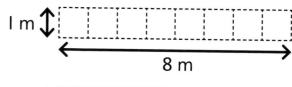

2 m

4 m

1 m × 8 m = 8 m²

2 m × 4 m = 8 m²

The length and width could either be 1 m × 8 m or 2 m × 4 m.

Think together

1 What is the area of this flower bed?

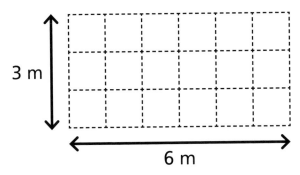

3 m

6 m

There are ☐ rows of metre squares.

Each row contains ☐ squares.

☐ × ☐ = ☐

There are ☐ metre squares altogether.

The area of the flower bed is ☐ m².

2 What is the area of this rectangle?

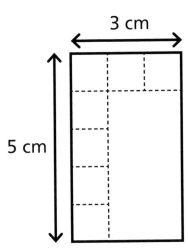

3 cm

5 cm

length × width = Area

☐ cm × ☐ cm = ☐ cm²

The area of this rectangle is ☐ cm².

3 How many different rectangles can you make that have an area of 24 cm²? Explain how you know.

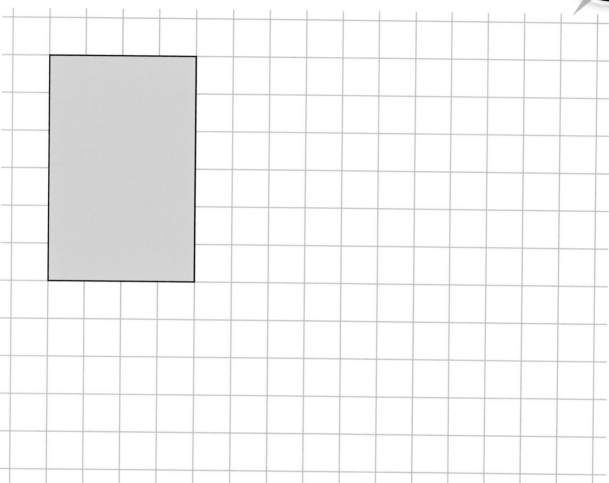

I am going to use a table to record my results.

I can think of a way to order them so we do not miss any out!

211

Comparing area

Discover

1 **a)** Which window has the larger area, A or B?

b) What is the area of window C in square metres (m²)?

Share

a) Each small pane of glass has an area of I square metre.

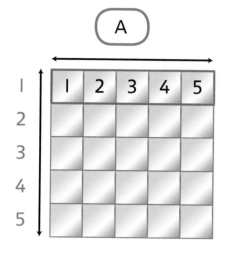

A

B

A has 5 rows of 5 panes

$5 \times 5 = 25$ panes

The area of window A is 25 m².

B has 3 rows of 8 panes

$3 \times 8 = 24$ panes

The area of window B is 24 m².

25 > 24, so window A has the larger area.

b)

I am going to use length × width to work out the area of window C.

C

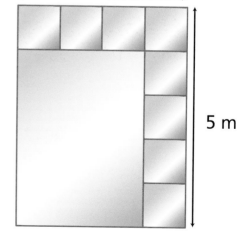

4 m

5 m

Area = length × width

Area of window C = 5 m × 4 m = 20 m

The area of window C is 20 m².

Think together

1 Which shape has the larger area?

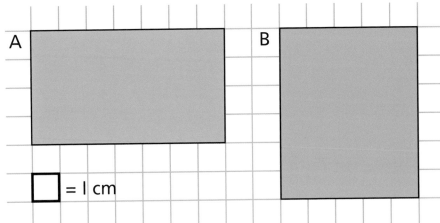

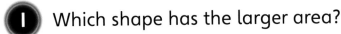

A   B

⬜ = 1 cm

Shape A has ⬜ rows of ⬜.   Shape B has ⬜ rows of ⬜.

⬜ × ⬜ = ⬜ cm²   ⬜ × ⬜ = ⬜ cm²

⬜ cm² > ⬜ cm²

Shape ⬜ has the larger area.

2 a) Use multiplication to find the area of these rectangles.

Area of X = ⬜ × ⬜ = ⬜ m²

Area of Y = ⬜ × ⬜ = ⬜ m²

Area of Z = ⬜ × ⬜ = ⬜ m²

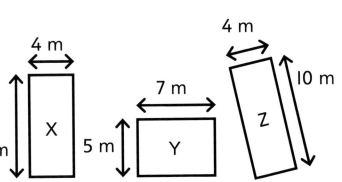

b) Using the letters X, Y, Z, order the rectangles from the largest to smallest area.

⬜ ⬜ ⬜

3 Kate and Aki have each drawn a rectangle.

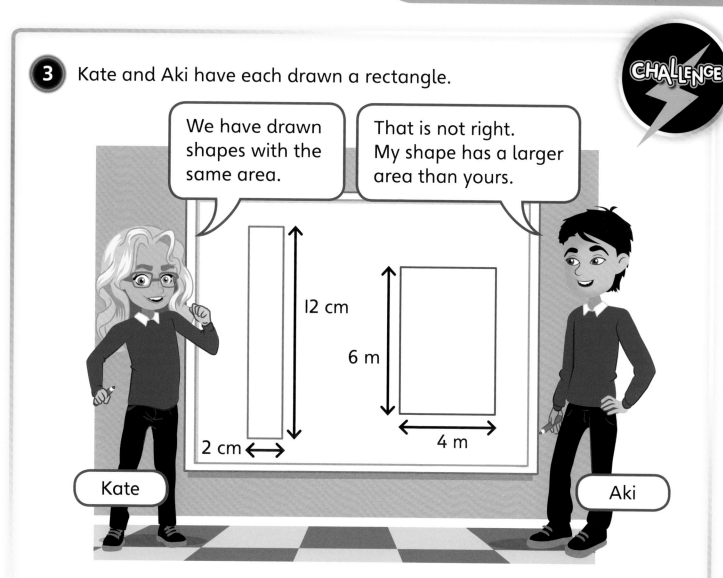

We have drawn shapes with the same area.

That is not right. My shape has a larger area than yours.

12 cm

6 m

2 cm

4 m

Kate

Aki

Who is correct?

Explain your answer.

I compared 2 × 12 with 4 × 6.

I looked at the units of measure too. That helped me answer the question.

215

Estimating area

Discover

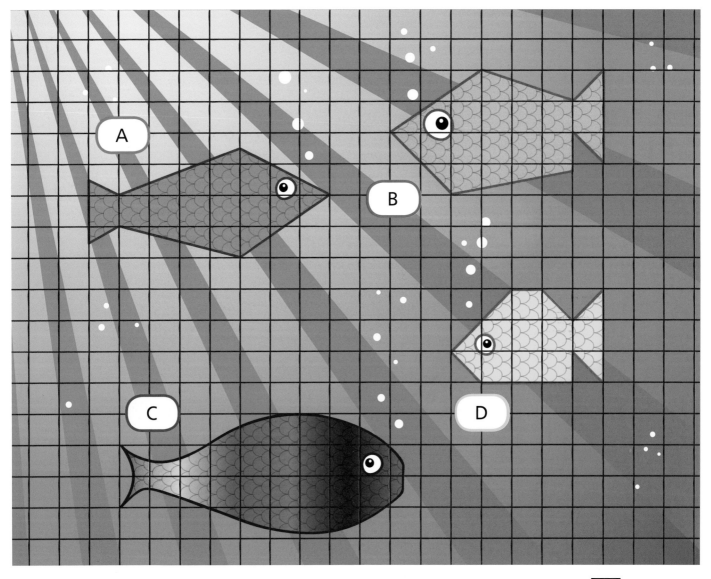

 = 1 cm²

1 **a)** How can you estimate the area of fish A?

b) Which fish has the largest area?

Share

a) When a shape is made of some whole squares and some part squares, you can estimate its area.

I am going to start by counting the whole squares.

Then we can think about the almost-whole squares, the half squares and those that are less than half.

There are 8 whole squares.

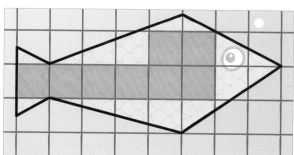

There are 6 almost-whole squares.

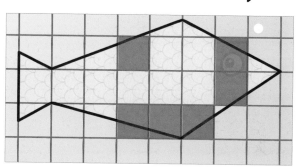

There is 1 half square.

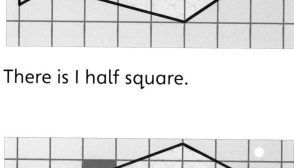

Ignore any squares that are less than half.

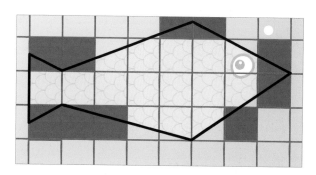

$8 + 6 + \frac{1}{2} + 0 = 14\frac{1}{2}$ squares

b)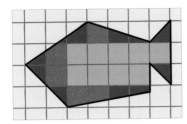

B   C   D

Fish	Whole squares	Almost-whole squares	Half squares	Estimated area (cm²)
B	9	5	7 (= $3\frac{1}{2}$ whole squares)	$17\frac{1}{2}$
D	10	8	6 (= 3 whole squares)	21
C	8	0	6 (= 3 whole squares)	11

Fish C has the largest area.

Think together

1 Estimate the area of this crab.

☐ whole squares

☐ almost-whole squares

☐ half squares = ☐ squares

☐ + ☐ + ☐ = ☐

The area of the crab is about ☐ squares.

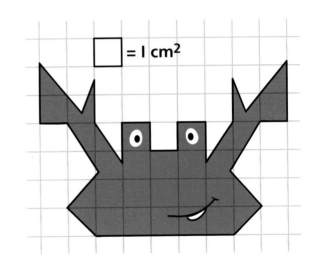

☐ = 1 cm²

2 Use a table to estimate the area of the sails on this boat.

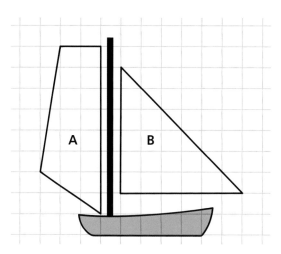

Sail	Whole squares	Almost-whole squares	Half squares	Less-than-half squares	Estimated area (squares)
A					
B					

3 Explain who you think is correct, Flo or Astrid.

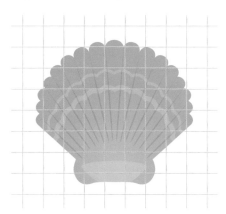

I want to count the squares that are less than half. They are part of the area too.

I think we should ignore them!

219

End of unit check

1 Use a ruler to measure the perimeter of this shape. What is it?

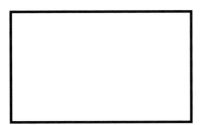

| **A** 5 cm | **B** 15 cm | **C** 8 cm | **D** 16 cm |

2 Which of these is not true?

A To find the perimeter of a rectangle, double the length and add it to double the width.

B To find the perimeter of a square, measure one side length and multiply it by 4.

C To find the perimeter of a rectangle, multiply the length by the width.

D To find the perimeter of a rectangle, measure each of the four sides and add them all together.

3 What is the perimeter of this field?

A 184 m

B 92 m

C 45 m

D 47 m

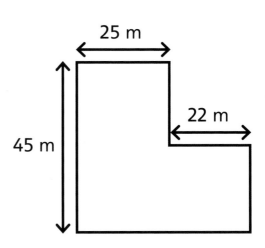

4 A square has a side length of 7 cm. What is its area?

    A 28 cm²   **B** 49 cm²   **C** 7 cm²   **D** 49 cm

5 What is the side marked A?

    A 3 m

    B 5 m

    C 7 m

    D 10 m

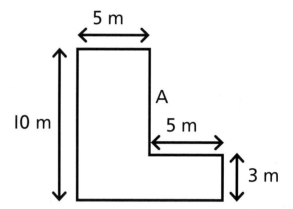

6 A gardener has planted a square flower bed in the middle of a square lawn.

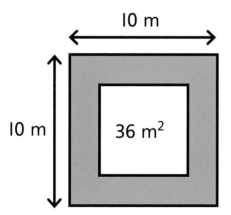

The flower bed has an area of 36 m².

The lawn is the shaded area on the diagram.

What is the area of the lawn?

 m²

→ **Practice book 5A p161**

Yes, we have! I enjoyed learning new methods.

What have we learnt?

Can you do all these things?

- ⚡ Understand place value up to 1,000,000
- ⚡ Count in 100,000s
- ⚡ Draw two-way tables and line graphs
- ⚡ Find factors and prime numbers
- ⚡ Calculate areas of rectangles

Some of it was difficult, but we did not give up!

Now you are ready for the next books!